SO-BRY-293

THE IMPACT OF
WORLD WAR I

INTERPRETATIONS OF AMERICAN HISTORY

John Higham and Bradford Perkins

EDITORS

THE IMPACT

of

WORLD WAR I

EDITED BY

ARTHUR S. LINK

PRINCETON UNIVERSITY

HARPER & ROW
Publishers
NEW YORK, EVANSTON, AND LONDON

LIBRARY
COLBY-SAWYER COLLEGE
NEW LONDON, NH 08257

E
780
.L48

For
Alpheus T. Mason

THE IMPACT OF WORLD WAR I
COPYRIGHT © 1969 BY ARTHUR S. LINK

Printed in the United States of America. All rights reserved. No part of this book may be used or reproduced in any manner whatsoever without written permission except in the case of brief quotations embodied in critical articles and reviews. For information address Harper & Row, Publishers, Incorporated, 49 East 33rd Street, New York, N.Y. 10016.

LIBRARY OF CONGRESS CATALOG CARD NUMBER: 69-18488

LIBRARY
99212

Contents

Editors' Introduction

This volume—and companions in the series, "Interpretations of American History"—makes a special effort to cope with one of the basic dilemmas confronting every student of history. On the one hand, historical knowledge shares a characteristic common to all appraisals of human affairs. It is partial and selective. It picks out some features and facts of a situation while ignoring others that may be equally pertinent. The more selective an interpretation is, the more memorable and widely applicable it can be. On the other hand, history has to provide what nothing else does: a total estimate, a multifaceted synthesis, of man's experience in particular times and places. To study history, therefore, is to strive simultaneously for a clear, selective focus and for an integrated, over-all view.

In that spirit, each volume of the series aims to resolve the varied literature on a major topic or event into a meaningful whole. One interpretation, we believe, does not deserve as much of a student's attention as another simply because they are in conflict. Instead of contriving a balance between opposing views, or choosing polemical material simply to create an appearance of controversy Professor Link has exercised his own judgment on the relative importance of different aspects or interpretations of a problem. We have asked him to select some of what he considers the best, most persuasive writings bearing on the impact of World War I on the American people, 1914–1920, indicating in the introductory essay and headnotes his reasons for considering these accounts convincing or significant. When appropriate, he has also brought out the relation between older and more recent approaches to the subject. The editor's own competence and experience in the field enable him to provide a sense of order and to indicate the evolution and complexity of interpretations. He is, then, like other editors in this series, an informed participant rather than a mere observer, a student sharing with other students the results of his own investigations of the literature on a crucial phase of American development.

John Higham
Bradford Perkins

INTRODUCTION

This is a book about the impact of World War I. Most historians agree that that awful conflict was a turning point or watershed in modern history, with more important repercussions, both immediate and long-range, for Europe than for the United States. Thus, we have to be more modest when we say that this is a book primarily about the impact of World War I upon the American people. As we shall see, it left a lasting imprint upon their position in world affairs, their domestic political economy, their constitutional traditions, and the very fabric of their social life.

The impact of the War fell most immediately upon the diplomatic policies of the United States. The country had been a great power for at least a generation before 1914. However, since its emergence to such status the United States government—reflecting deeply felt popular convictions—had remained stubbornly aloof from European controversies, with the single possible exception of President Theodore Roosevelt's participation in the first Moroccan crisis of 1906; and Roosevelt's intervention in this affair had been more private than public.

Aloofness and unconcern simply were not viable postures for President Woodrow Wilson and his advisers once the holocaust enveloped Europe and spread to the Far East in 1914. The United States was the richest and most powerful of the neutral countries. It had worldwide trade and interests that were bound to be affected by belligerent policies. Its actions in response to these policies would have considerable bearing of their own on the outcome of the War.

Wilson's first response—a proclamation of official neutrality—was inevitable, given the division among the American people regarding the rival alliances and the general determination to avoid involvement if at all possible. But Wilson did more than proclaim neutrality. Turning aside from his preoccupation with domestic issues and the diplomatic problems of the Western hemisphere, the President devoted his prodigious talents and energies to the defense of American neutral rights, principally rights of trade and travel, against both the challenge of the British cruiser and the threat of the German submarine.

In his role as principal champion of neutral rights, Wilson emerged as one of the leading actors on the stage of world affairs between the outbreak of the War in August, 1914, and the early months of 1917, when events would cause a sudden change in American policy. Moreover, his decisions during the period of American neutrality were crucial for the belligerents. Wilson's judgment that the Allied blockade of the Central Powers was basically legal, and therefore acceptable, stimulated an enormous trade that made it possible for the Allies to maintain their war effort. This war trade, incidentally, also soon brought roaring prosperity to the United States. Wilson's decision to oppose some German practices, such as submarine attacks against unarmed passenger ships, but to accept a cruiser-type submarine war against maritime commerce, benefited the Germans and helped to maintain the military equilibrium that had prevailed between the two sides after the Allies turned back the German thrust toward Paris in the First Battle of the Marne.

The defense of neutral rights was, along with isolation from European entanglements, the oldest tradition in American foreign policy. The War's most significant impact upon American diplomacy was the change that it prompted in policies toward Europe. Moved by a humanitarian desire to end the war, and encouraged from time to time by the British government, Wilson took steps to stop the conflict through his own mediation. More important, he announced that the United States was willing to join a postwar league of nations and help to preserve the peace of the world in the future. These actions thrust Wilson on to the center of the world stage. As we can see in perspective, they also marked a fundamental reversal of American foreign policy. The American people later repudiated Wilsonian policies, but it was never really possible for them to return to a prewar type of isolation because of what Wilson had done.

The German decision in January, 1917, to bid for victory through a wholesale assault against all maritime commerce wrecked Wilson's mediation efforts and forced the United States into the War in April, 1917. Even so, Wilson continued to be the principal spokesman for peace even while he waged war. His statements of war aims, particularly his Fourteen Points Address of January 8, 1918, made him the leading spokesman in the world for those forces wanting an end to imperialism, rival alliances, and arms races—the "old diplomacy"—and, instead, the construction of a new international community based upon disarmament, open diplomacy, the development of colonial peoples, the right of self-determination for minorities, and the policies of friendship instead of war.

After Germany was defeated in November, 1918, Wilson went in person to the Paris Peace Conference to fight for a just settlement and a League of Nations that would enforce a liberal peace of understanding. In retrospect, it is clear that Wilson was the commanding figure among the notables who gathered in Paris in January, 1919. It is also clear that he did succeed at Paris, in spite of the number of concessions that he had to make, in building a new international structure that could prove capable of correcting the injustices of the Versailles Treaty and of forming the basis for a new international order that could avoid both extremes of the predatory old diplomacy and the new revolutionary communism.

Meanwhile, the impact in the United States of the experience of mobilizing for a major war effort had been profound. In one sense, the War saw the first full flowering of the American progressive movement. For a generation, progressives had urged the expansion of governmental power, particularly of federal power, to cope with the social and economic problems raised by the combination of financial and industrial interests and by the exploitation of disadvantaged classes like women, children, and workers in general. Progressives had achieved many of their goals before 1917 under Theodore Roosevelt and Wilson. But the sheer necessities attendant upon mobilizing, and mobilizing rapidly, for total war produced a far greater expansion of federal authority than most progressives would have dreamed possible in 1916. To state the result briefly, the entire economic life of the nation was harnessed for purposeful action. Better still—from the progressive point of view—was the fact that the federal government seemed as determined to win democracy at home as it was to make democracy safe abroad—by heavy taxes on wealth, support for collective bargaining by organized labor, and new experiments in social legislation and action.

As it turned out, the mobilization of men and economic resources was not enough to fight a total war. It was necessary to mobilize hearts and minds as well. And under George Creel and his Committee on Public Information, the government launched what was undoubtedly the largest and most effective propaganda campaign in American history. At the same time that it was trying to convert the numerous opponents of participation in the War, the government, in the Espionage Act of June 15, 1917, sought to prevent open opposition to the draft and the war effort in general. Egged on by a growing anti-German hysteria and by a fear of domestic radicals, Congress, in April, 1918, approved the Sedition Act outlawing *any* overt opposition to the government and its policies.

There were numerous spy scares, many outcroppings of anti-German hysteria, and sustained drives against opponents of the war such as the Socialist party and the Industrial Workers of the World. And all the while, conservatives deliberately used the Espionage and Sedition Acts, and state legislation as well, to attack so-called radicals, such as those in the midwestern Nonpartisan League, pacifists, and so on.

The greatest and most lasting impact of this campaign of repression was the permanent erosion of ancient American liberties of unbridled free speech. The Supreme Court, in *Schenck v. United States*, 1919, upheld the Espionage Act on the ground that the federal government had the right to punish utterances that might constitute a "clear and present" danger. In *Abrams v. United States*, 1919, the Court soon confirmed the Schenck decision in a ruling that gave the government virtually unlimited power over speech during wartime. Thus, the "clear and present" danger doctrine was firmly embedded in American judicial doctrine, to be resurrected later, most notably in the early 1950s, when Communists were convicted and imprisoned for alleged advocacy of the forcible overthrow of the government.

Mass hysteria, such as the American people experienced against Germans and German-Americans, is more easily started than ended. Hysteria continued unabated for at least a year and a half after the Armistice. Part of it was directed against Negroes and led to the worst outbreak of anti-Negro rioting since Reconstruction days. But most of the anti-German sentiment turned into an unreasoning fear of Communists. Fed by bomb scares, labor unrest, and the organization of American Communist parties in 1919, this fear resulted in local witch hunts, the refusal by the New York legislature to seat Socialist members simply because they were members of the Socialist party, and the casting of a nationwide dragnet of assorted radicals by Attorney General A. Mitchell Palmer in early January, 1920.

There were signs of very strong life in what Arno J. Mayer of Princeton University has called the "forces of movement," even while the nation was being convulsed by the Red Scare. Organized labor, determined to preserve wartime gains, was making plans for organizational drives in the mass industries. Progressives and liberals, intoxicated by the vision of preserving and extending wartime controls, were demanding new welfare programs, social insurance, and a peacetime guarantee of labor's right to organize and to share in profits. For a time in 1919 it seemed that the nation stood on the verge of a significant forward movement of progressivism.

In fact, progressives did win several notable victories in the aftermath of postwar idealism—the federal prohibition and woman suffrage amendments, new conservation legislation, a measure for definitive regulation of railroads, and the statutory limitation of immigration, among other things. However, the time was unpropitious for the type of legislation that the more advanced social reformers were demanding. To begin with, there was a general reaction against strict wartime controls in the United States as there was in the western European countries. More important, conservatives were able to exploit the anti-Communist hysteria in turning back organized labor, particularly in the American Federation of Labor's drive to organize the steel industry, and in tarring reformers in general with communism.

Ironically, Woodrow Wilson, who had raised progressive hopes so high, made one of the principal contributions to the failure of progressives to organize a strong and successful coalition in 1919–1920.

Like the Red Scare, Wilson's domestic failure was also brought on by the War. The President's preoccupation with problems of the peace and his prolonged absence from the United States prevented him from giving any leadership at home during the critical period of demobilization. While Wilson debated in Paris, the great machinery of mobilization was dismantled, and events were permitted to drift at home. Then Wilson's long, hard campaign for the ratification of the Versailles Treaty broke his health and removed him from the political arena in 1920. Moreover, his absolute insistence upon ratification of the Treaty without important reservations alienated large portions of his followers and subordinated domestic issues to the single issue of the League of Nations during the Presidential campaign of 1920. While Wilson's coalition crumbled and his followers were in disarray, conservative Republicans were able to unite in opposition both to the League of Nations and so-called radicalism, and to sweep to victory under Warren G. Harding in 1920.

Yet it would be naïve to repeat the old cliché that the chief impact of the War was to kill progressivism and the Wilsonian dream of American leadership in building a new liberal international community. The important fact was that the United States would never be the same again because of the experiences of the American people during World War I. Out of the ferment of wartime idealism came a host of proposals for social and economic reform that would germinate during the 1920s and find full legislative expression during the New Deal era within the brief span of some fifteen years. Moreover, when Americans were once again confronted by a dire national emergency—the Great Depression—they would turn for solutions to the mobilization of 1917–1918 and for leaders to the very men who had guided the country during the same period.

Finally, Americans, as much as they complained, found during the 1920s and 1930s that there was no escaping the challenges of international leadership. Wilson, in his advocacy of American leadership in an effective collective security system, was simply a generation ahead of his time. Even in defeat he inspired a future generation of leaders, laid the foundations for a new international order, and presented the challenges to which Americans would finally respond in the 1940s.

The foregoing has been said merely by way of introduction, in order to provide a general historical context for the articles and excerpts which follow and which will illustrate in detail the themes just adumbrated.

Wilson and the Struggle
for Neutrality

ARTHUR S. LINK

In the following selection, the editor describes the impact of the outbreak of the European war on the American people and the Wilson Administration. Challenging interpretations current in the 1930s among so-called revisionist historians, the editor argues that the President struggled hard, and on the whole successfully, to establish and defend American neutrality before 1917. In particular, he describes the flexibility—the combination of moral principle and tactical pragmatism—which marked Wilson's policies, but which is so often overlooked. He also discusses the motivation behind Wilson's first mediation project, the so-called House-Grey Memorandum.

The entire selection suggests interesting questions: Is it the duty of a "neutral" to manage his affairs so that his efforts contribute equally to both sides in the war from which he abstains? Or is it his duty to treat each belligerent equally, allowing geographical and economic factors free play? Is it conceivable that the former type of neutrality—impartial impact constructed by discriminatory policy—could actually be worked out?

From Arthur S. Link, *Wilson the Diplomatist: A Look at His Major Foreign Policies*, Baltimore: The Johns Hopkins Press, 1957, pp. 31–60. Reprinted by permission of the publisher. The original footnotes in this selection have been omitted.

For Woodrow Wilson and the American people, who had a positive disinclination to play the game of power politics, events on the international stage intruded in an ironic if fateful way from 1914 to 1917. By the spring of 1915 the United States was the only great power not directly involved in the war then raging from western Europe to the Far East. Desiring only to deal fairly with both sides and to avoid military involvement, the President soon found that neutrality, as well as war, has its perplexities and perils.

• • •

Among the most pervasive pressures controlling Wilson's decisions throughout the period 1914–1917 were the attitudes and opinions of the American people concerning the war and America's proper relation to it. Few presidents in American history have been more keenly aware of risks that the leader runs when he ceases to speak for the preponderant majority. "The ear of the leader must ring with the voices of the people. He cannot be of the school of the prophets; he must be of the number of those who studiously serve the slow-paced daily need." Thus Wilson had written in 1890; thus he believed and practiced while formulating his policies toward the belligerents in the First World War.

The dominant American sentiment throughout the period of nonintervention can be summarily characterized by the single adjective "neutral." This is not to say that Americans had no opinions on the merits of the war and the claims of the opposing alliances, or that there were no differences among the popular reactions. It is simply to state the fairly obvious fact that the preponderant majority, whose opinions played a decisive role in shaping Wilson's policies, did not believe that their interests and security were vitally involved in the outcome of the war and desired to avoid participation if that were possible without sacrificing rights that should not be yielded. The prevalence and astounding vitality of neutralism, in spite of the severest provocations and all the efforts of propagandists on both sides, formed at once the unifying principle of American politics and the compelling reality with which Wilson had to deal from 1914 to 1917.

On the other hand, it would be a large error to imply that Wilson was a prisoner of the public opinion of the majority, and that his will to adopt sterner policies toward one group of belligerents or the other was paralyzed by the stronger counterforce of neutralism. Actually, the evidence points overwhelmingly to the conclusion that Wilson personally shared the opinions of the majority, in brief, that he was substantially neutral in attitude, and that his policies were controlled as much by his own convictions as by the obvious wishes of the people.

Never once throughout the period of American neutrality did Wilson explain by word of mouth or set down in writing his personal views on the causes and merits of the war. However, this does not mean that one is entirely helpless in trying to reconstruct his methods of thinking and the character of his thought about this subject. There is some direct and considerably more circumstantial evidence to indicate that he set up certain general principles and assumptions at the outset and reasoned deductively from them to form his conclusions.

One of these assumptions was Wilson's belief that the causes of the war were enormously complex and obscure. The conflict, he believed, had its origins in the divisive nationalisms of the Austro-Hungarian Empire, in Russia's drive for free access to the Mediterranean, in France's longing for the recovery of Alsace-Lorraine, in Germany's challenge to Britain's naval and commercial supremacy, in the system of rival alliances that had grown up following the Franco-Prussian War, and in the general imperialistic rivalries of the late nineteenth and early twentieth centuries. At no time in correspondence or conversation did he ever say, "These are the important root causes of the war." Nevertheless, he revealed conclusively that he thought that they were when he first singled them out as prime causes of international conflict that would have to be removed if the world were ever to achieve a lasting peace.

It followed in Wilson's mind, then, that all the belligerents shared to some degree in the responsibility for the war and that one could not ascribe all blame to one side or the other. Nor could one use simple explanations in talking about conflicting war objectives. It was clear to Wilson that all the belligerents sincerely believed that they were fighting for their existence, but that all of them desired a smashing victory in order to enhance their power, win new territory, and impose crushing indemnities upon their enemies. Because this was true, Wilson reasoned, the best kind of settlement would be a stalemate in which neither alliance would have the power to impose terms upon the other.

In his fundamental thinking about war in general, moreover, Wilson shared in a remarkable way the assumptions of the majority of Americans. Like most of his fellow-citizens, he abhorred the very thought of using violence to achieve national objectives; indeed, he was reluctant to use even the threat of force in diplomacy. Like the Socialists, independent radicals, and a large majority of southern and western farmers, he suspected that the financiers and industrialists favored preparedness and a strong foreign policy in order to increase profits and provoke a war that would end the reform movement at home. Like the majority of Americans, he was willing to think of fighting only as a last resort and then only as a means of defending rights that no civilized nation could yield.

Fortified by these convictions, Wilson struggled hard and on the whole successfully to be impartial in thought as well as in deed, as he had asked the American people at the outbreak of the war to do. In fact, he succeeded in this impossible undertaking far better than most of his contemporaries and his historical critics. His method was to rely upon the general assumptions that he was sure were sound and then virtually to seal himself off from the passionate arguments and indictments of partisans of either alliance, by simply refusing to listen to them. "I recall," Secretary Lansing afterward wrote, for example, "that . . . his attitude toward evidence of German atrocities in Belgium and toward accounts of the horrors of submarine warfare . . . [was that] he would not read of them and showed anger if the details were called to his attention."

This does not mean that Wilson was able completely to subordinate emotional reactions and personal feelings. Like the majority of Americans, he was to a degree pro-British; on two, perhaps three, occasions during the two and a half years of American neutrality he avowed to close friends his personal sympathy for the Allied cause. But it would be a difficult task to prove that Wilson's pro-British sympathies were ever controlling or indeed even very strong. At no time did he act like a man willing to take measures merely to help his supposed friends. On the contrary, all his policies were aimed either at averting American participation on Britain's side or at ending the war on terms that would have denied the spoils of victory to Britain and her allies. If this is too big an assertion to be taken on faith, then perhaps the reasons for making it will become apparent as we see the way in which Wilson executed policies toward the two leading antagonists.

All authorities, whether friendly or hostile to Wilson, would agree that the acid tests of his neutrality were the policies that he worked out and applied vis-à-vis the British from 1914 to 1917. He has been most condemned by that group of historians highly censorious of his policies, generally known as revisionists, on this score—for becoming the captive of pro-Allied influences within his administration, for condoning such sweeping British control of neutral commerce that the Germans were forced to resort to drastic countermeasures, for permitting American prosperity to become dependent upon loans and exports to the Allies, in short, for permitting a situation to develop that made it inevitable that the United States would go to war if the success of Allied arms was ever seriously threatened.

Like most fallacious arguments, this one contains a certain element of plausibility. Wilson did condone a far-reaching British maritime system. American neutrality did work greatly to the benefit of the Allies. The error arises in saying that these things occurred because Wilson and his advisers necessarily wanted them to occur.

Perhaps the best way to gain a clear understanding of why Anglo-American relations developed as they did from 1914 to 1917 is to see how the policies that decisively shaped those relations emerged in several stages in response to certain pressures, events, and forces. The first stage, lasting from August, 1914, to about August, 1915, was in many ways the most critical, because the basic American response to the war and to the British maritime system was formulated then. That response was governed in the first instance by two domestic realities: the overwhelming, virtually unanimous, American desire to be neutral, and the pressures in the United States for a large measure of free trade with Britain's enemies.

In view of the prevailing American sentiment at the outbreak of the war, a policy of strict official neutrality was the only possible course for the United States government. This fact prompted the President's official proclamations of neutrality, supplemented by his appeal to the American people for impartiality in thought; the subsequent working out by the State Department of the elaborate technical rules to preserve American neutrality; and the establishment of a Joint State and Navy Neutrality Board to advise the various departments upon the correct interpretation of international law.

One cannot read the records revealing how these policies were formulated without being convinced that their authors were high-minded in their determination to be fair to both sides. Indeed, Wilson and the man who chiefly influenced him in the formulation of the rules of neutrality, Secretary of State Bryan, were so intent upon being fair to the Germans that they adopted policies during the first months of the war that were highly disadvantageous to the British, if not unneutral. One was to prevent the sale of submarine parts, and hence parts for any naval craft, by a private American firm to the British government, on the ground that such a sale would be "contrary to . . . strict neutrality." Wilson persisted in supporting Bryan in this matter, in spite of advice from Counselor Lansing and the Joint Neutrality Board to the effect that their position was contrary to international law.

Infinitely more damaging to the Allies was the administration's second effort to lean over backward in being "strictly" neutral—the ban of loans by American bankers to the belligerent governments that the President permitted Bryan to impose in August, 1914. From a technical viewpoint, the ban was not unneutral, but it was highly prejudicial to the Allies because its effect was potentially to deny them their otherwise legal right to purchase supplies in the American market. These two incidents are not to be understood as revealing any anti-British bias on the part of Wilson and Bryan, although British officials at the time were convinced that they did. I mention them only to show what an important role the administration's desire to be impartial played in the formation of policies vis-à-vis the British during the early period of American neutrality.

The other pressure shaping American policies at this time was the force of combined demands at home for the virtually free transit of American ships and goods to the European neutrals and the belligerent Central Powers. So powerful were these demands, especially from cotton growers and exporters and their spokesmen in Congress, that Wilson personally sponsored two measures highly disadvantageous to the British and unneutral in fact as well as in spirit. One was a change in the ship registry law, put into effect by an act approved August 18, 1914, which made it easy for German or other foreign shipping firms to take out American registry for their vessels. The other was a plan to establish a federal corporation to purchase German ships in American ports and to use them to carry supplies to the belligerents, particularly to Germany. Wilson applied heavy pressure to obtain congressional approval of this, the so-called ship-purchase bill, during the short term from December, 1914, to March, 1915; he failed only because of a stout senatorial filibuster.

In negotiations with the British government during the early months of the war, Wilson fought hard in response to domestic pressures to keep the channels of international commerce open to American ships and goods. He did not go as far in defense of neutral rights as some of his predecessors, but he did suggest a code so sweeping that an enforcement of it would have meant almost total destruction of the British system of maritime controls. Specifically, the President first proposed on August 6, 1914, that the belligerents adopt the rules of naval warfare laid down in the Declaration of London of 1909, a convention never ratified by Great Britain or the United States, which permitted the free transit of all good except those obviously contraband. When the British rejected this suggestion, the President came back on October 16, proposing a compromise that would have still seriously impaired the effectiveness of British sea power. When this effort also failed, Wilson then announced that his government would assert and defend all its rights under international law and treaties.

I have described these policies and proposals because they so clearly reveal Wilson's neutral intentions and what he would have done in matters of trade had he been able to make the rules himself. But he obviously could not follow his personal preferences alone or respond only to domestic pressures. In seeking to assert and defend American neutral rights he ran head-on into a reality as important as the reality of the pressures at home. It was the British determination to use sea power to prevent American ships and goods from going to the sustenance of the German economy and military forces.

British assumption of a nearly absolute control of the seas washing western Europe began with relatively mild measures in August, 1914, and culminated in the suppression of virtually all commerce to the Central Powers in March, 1915. For the British, this was not a question of adhering to the laws of blockade or of violating them, or of doing things merely to be nice to American friends. It was a question of achieving their supreme objective, to deprive their enemies of vital raw materials and goods, without risking the alienation of the United States. The controlling fact for the British was the necessity of preserving American friendship, in order to assure the uninterrupted rhythm of the North Atlantic trade. As the British Foreign Secretary [Sir Edward Grey] at the time frankly put it:

Blockade of Germany was essential to the victory of the Allies, but the ill-will of the United States meant their certain defeat. . . . It was better therefore to carry on the war without blockade, if need be, than to incur a break with the United States about contraband and thereby deprive the Allies of the resources necessary to carry on the war at all or with any chance of success. The object of diplomacy, therefore, was to secure the maximum of blockade that could be enforced without a rupture with the United States.

The crucial question all along, therefore, was whether the United States, the only neutral power strong enough successfully to challenge the British measures, would acquiesce or resist to the point of threatening or using force. The American response during the formative period of neutrality was, in brief, to accept the British system and to limit action against it to a vigorous assertion of American legal rights for future adjudication. All this is too well known to require any further exposition. What is not so well understood are the reasons why Wilson and his advisers acquiesced in a solution that denied the objectives that they and a large segment of the American public demanded. These reasons may be briefly summarized, as follows:

First, the British maritime system, in spite of American allegations to the contrary, enjoyed the advantage of being legitimate and usually legal, or nearly so, by traditional criteria. It was legitimate rather than fraudulent, and legal rather than capricious or terroristic, in its major aspects because the British did in fact hold undisputed sea supremacy and were therefore able to execute their controls in an orderly fashion. In asserting their own rights, the Americans could not well deny the advantages that accrued to the British by virtue of their sea power. The British, for example, had an undoubted right to establish a blockade of the Central Powers, and the American attempt to persuade the London government to use techniques effective only in the days of the sailing ship did not have much cogency in the twentieth century.

Second, much of the success of the British in establishing their control depended upon the way in which they went about it. Had they instituted their total blockade at the outset of the war, the American reaction would undoubtedly have been violent. Instead, the British applied their controls gradually, with a careful eye upon American opinion, using the opportunities provided by recurrent crises in German-American relations to institute their severest measures.

Third, the British were careful never to offend so many American interests at one time that retaliation would have been inevitable, or any single interest powerful enough by itself to compel retaliation. There was the case of cotton, which the officials in London were determined to prevent from going to Germany because it was an ingredient of gunpowder. Not until a year after the war began did they put cotton on the list of absolute contraband; even then they went to the extraordinary length of underwriting the entire American cotton market in order to avert an irresistible southern pressure in Congress for retaliation. In addition, although they were ruthless in enforcing their blockade, the British took careful pains to avoid any serious injury to American property interests. They confiscated only the most obvious contraband; in all doubtful cases they paid value for cargoes or ships seized. Their objective was to control, not to destroy, American commerce.

Fourth, there was great significance in the language and symbolism that the British Foreign Office used in defending the measures of the Admiralty and Ministry of Blockade. By justifying their maritime system in terms of international law and the right of retaliation, and (at least before the summer of 1916) by making an honest effort to meet American objections half way when possible, the British made it almost inevitable that the Washington authorities would have to reply in the same language, thus giving a purely *legal* character to the issues of sovereignty and inherent national rights. The significance of this achievement can be seen in the conviction of Wilson and the majority of Americans that the Anglo-American disputes did involve only property rights, which should be vindicated only by an appeal to much-controverted international law. Moreover, by appealing to the American government and people in the name of friendship and by always professing their devotion to the cause of humanity, the British succeeded in evoking strong feelings of sympathy and understanding on the other side of the water.

Finally, the British were able partially to justify their own blockade measures as legitimate adaptations to a changing technology by pointing to precedents established by the Washington government itself during the American Civil War. To be sure, the British drew some incorrect analogies (as Lansing pointed out) between American and British practice; even so, their main contention—that the American government had also stretched the rules of blockade to allow for technological changes—was essentially correct.

Wilson's refusal to challenge the British maritime system, in short, to break the British blockade, was almost inevitable in view of the facts we have just reviewed, *if the President's objective was simply to maintain as best he could the neutral position of the United States.* An absolute neutrality was in any event impossible because of the total character of the war and America's importance in the world economy. It often happened that any action by the United States inevitably conferred a benefit on one side and thereby injured the other, at least indirectly. In these circumstances, neutrality often consisted of doing the things that would give the least unwarranted or undeserved advantages.

By this standard, it would have been more unneutral than neutral for Wilson to have broken the British maritime system by enforcing highly doubtful technical rights under international law. Judged by practical standards rather than by the often conflicting criteria of neutrality, Wilson's acceptance of the British system seems realistic and wise—indeed, the only choice that he could have made in the circumstances. This is true because the results of destroying the British blockade would have been the wrecking of American friendship with the two great European democracies and the probable victory of the Central Powers, without a single compensating gain for the interests and security of the United States. Only the sure achievement of some great political objective like a secure peace settlement, certainly not the winning of a commercial advantage or the defense of doubtful neutral rights, would have justified Wilson in undertaking a determined challenge to British sea power.

The second stage in Anglo-American relations, lasting from the summer of 1915 to the late spring of 1916, saw the development of the natural economic consequence of the American adjustment to tightening British control of the seas. That consequence was the burgeoning of an enormous war trade between the United States and the Allies. The United States became the storehouse and armory of the Allies neither because there was any conspiracy on the part of certain pro-Allied leaders in Washington to make American prosperity dependent upon an Allied victory, nor because American businessmen and bankers were willing to incur the risks of war in order to increase their profits. The United States became the storehouse of the Allies for the simple reason that Great Britain and not Germany controlled the seas.

The war trade itself was entirely neutral. Indeed, any action by the United States government to impede it, unless undertaken for overriding political motives, would have been grossly prejudicial and unneutral. If it had been permitted to develop in a normal way, this commerce would have raised no important problems in the relations of the United States with the Allies. A problem of the first magnitude did arise, however, because the President, in the summer of 1914, had permitted Secretary Bryan to enforce his own private moral views by imposing a ban on loans by American bankers to the belligerents.

There was no difficulty so long as the British and French governments could find gold and dollars to settle their adverse trade balances. By the summer of 1915, however, Allied gold and dollar resources were near the point of exhaustion; and American insistence upon a continuation of cash payments could result only in gravely damaging the Allied economies and ending the North Atlantic trade altogether. Chedit could be found only in the United States, but credit meant floating loans, and loans to the belligerents were as much a political as an economic question because of the existence of Bryan's ban.

It is well known that the State Department under Bryan's direction substantially relaxed its credit embargo during the spring of 1915 and that Wilson and Bryan's successor, Lansing, lifted the ban altogether a few months later, at a time when the credit needs of the Allied governments were demonstrably acute. Even though the full facts bearing upon this matter have been available to scholars for more than twenty years, the reason for the administration's reversal are still not properly understood.

Bryan's ban could not survive the development of the war trade on a large scale because, in the first place, it (like the Embargo of 1808) was potentially nearly as disastrous to the United States as to the Allies. American material well-being was in large measure dependent upon foreign trade, and particularly upon trade with the Allied world. Such trade was possible during wartime only if American businessmen were willing to do for the Allies what they always did for solvent customers in temporary straits, namely, sell them goods on credit.

The most important reason that Bryan's embargo could not survive, however, was that it was an essentially unneutral policy that impeded the growth of the chief economic consequence of American neutrality, the legitimate war trade. The credit embargo and the war trade could not both survive. The former gave way because Wilson finally realized that it would be as unneutral to interfere with the extension of credit as it would be to stop the flow of goods. Bryan's ban was in a sense, therefore, a casualty chiefly of American neutrality.

The historian can talk himself blue in the face without really convincing his listeners that these simple facts are true. He can point out that Britain's existence depended upon her ability to use sea power to keep the channels of trade and credit open, just as Germany's existence depended upon the use of superior land power. He can demonstrate that the sale of goods and the extension of credit to belligerents by private parties were neutral in theory, tradition, and practice. He can show that the effect of unwarranted interference with such intercourse would have been seriously to penalize sea power to the advantage of land power. But a historian arguing this way makes little impression upon an American audience, because the issue is still too supercharged with emotionalism and is still resolved within a framework of economic determinism, of hostility to the business and financial classes, and of moralistic pacifism.

The second stage in Anglo-American relations witnessed the apparent convergence of the diplomatic policies of the two countries on the high level. During the summer and autumn of 1915 Colonel Edward M. House, Wilson's confidant and principal adviser on foreign policy, conceived a plan by which the American and British leaders would join hands to press for an end of the war through Wilson's mediation. The British Foreign Secretary, Sir Edward Grey, replied that his government would cooperate only if the Washington administration were willing to go beyond simple mediation and would agree to join a postwar international organization established for the purpose of effecting disarmament, maintaining freedom of the seas, and preserving peace. Wilson hopefully consented, and House went to Berlin, Paris, and London in January, 1916, to lay the diplomatic basis of mediation.

In London, House worked out in documentary form with Grey and the other members of the British Cabinet the specific terms of Anglo-American co-operation. Initialed by House and Grey on February 22, 1916, and known as the House-Grey Memorandum or Agreement, this document declared that President Wilson was ready, upon hearing from England and France that the time was ripe, to propose that a conference be called to end the war. Should the Allies accept and Germany refuse the invitation, the United States would "probably" enter the war against Germany. Should the conference meet and Germany refuse to accept a reasonable settlement, then the United States would also "probably" enter the war on the Allied side.

To the so-called revisionists the conclusion of the House Grey Agreement is irrefutable proof that Wilson had abandoned neutrality and meant to take the country into war at the first opportunity. To remove all doubt that this was true, they point to what happened during the weeks immediately following the initialing of the agreement.

While House had been carrying his negotiations in London to a successful conclusion, Wilson and Lansing had undertaken to avert the possibility of conflict with Germany over the issue of submarine attacks against armed merchantmen by proposing that the Allies disarm their merchant ships and that U-boats follow the old rules of cruiser warfare in attacking them. Using the President's suggestion as a pretext, the German authorities announced on February 10, 1916, that submarines would attack *armed* enemy merchantmen without warning after February 29. Then without warning Wilson and Lansing reversed themselves and announced that the American government would insist upon the right of Americans to travel on ships defensively armed and would hold the German government to strict account for the loss of any American lives on armed merchantmen. Adhering doggedly to this position in the face of a threatened rebellion in Congress, the President proceeded to use the opportunity afforded by the torpedoing without warning of the French Channel packet *Sussex* by a German submarine, "in contravention of earlier pledges," to threaten a break in diplomatic relations with Germany and to force the Imperial government to make sweeping concessions in its conduct of submarine warfare.

To the revisionist critics, the case is so clear that it needs no further proof. The House-Grey Agreement, they say, was conceived and concluded for the purpose of promoting early American intervention. Wilson at once sought to accomplish this goal by taking a position on armed merchant ships that was bound to provoke a crisis with Germany, and by pressing the German government so hard during the *Sussex* controversy that a break in relations would probably ensue. The plan failed, the revisionists explain, only because the violent opposition in Congress convinced the President that the lawmakers would never approve a declaration of war to uphold the right of Americans to travel on belligerent armed merchant ships, and only because the German authorities proved to be more conciliatory than Wilson had expected.

The revisionists are correct in asserting that the conclusion of the House-Grey Agreement marked the beginning of a new and epochal phase in Wilson's policies toward the belligerents. Otherwise they have missed the entire meaning of the affair, for the House-Grey Agreement was in Wilson's purpose *not an instrument of intervention, but a means of averting American involvement.* The truth of this important generalization will perhaps become evident when we recall the realities of the

American diplomatic situation during late 1915 and early 1916, and when we understand Wilson's motives and intentions in devising a solution.

The overshadowing reality confronting the makers of American foreign policy at this time was the grave possibility of war with Germany over the submarine issue. . . . It speeded the American acquiescence in the British maritime system. Most important, it prompted the President and his advisers to search for ways to avert the rupture that might draw the United States into the maelstrom.

One way out of the predicament was to come to a full understanding with the German government over the issues involved in the submarine controversy. This is what Lansing attempted to do and almost succeeded in accomplishing during his negotiations over the *Lusitania* affair. Another way out and a surer means of averting the peril of American involvement in the future was to bring the war itself to an end through Wilson's mediation. It seemed at the time that the best hope of peace lay in Anglo-American co-operation for a peace of compromise, specifically in the kind of co-operation detailed in the House-Grey Agreement.

Thus, Wilson approved this plan of mediation, but with a full realization that certain obligations and risks were involved. There was the necessity of giving positive assurances to the Allies, for they would have been at a fatal disadvantage in a peace conference without American support, in view of the strategic advantages that the Germans then enjoyed on the Continent of Europe. There was, moreover, the risk of war if the Germans refused to approve an armistice or proved to be unreasonable at a peace conference after agreeing to end the fighting. However, Wilson gave the necessary assurances in the belief that the risk of war involved was insignificant as compared to the greater danger of hostilities with Germany if he could not somehow bring the war to an end. This, then, was his dominant motive in sending House to Europe in January, 1916, and in approving the House-Grey Agreement at the cost of Lansing's proposed compromise for submarine warfare.

In the final analysis, our judgment of Wilson's mediation plans must depend upon the kind of settlement that he had in mind and for which he was willing to run the risk of war in order to achieve peace. It is clear that Wilson envisaged a "reasonable" settlement based upon recognition that the war was a stalemate and upon a return for the most part of the *status quo ante bellum*. It meant, Wilson also hoped, the kind of settlement in which all the belligerents would forego annexations and indemnities, put aside past differences, and join hands with the United States to create a new international order. In his final discussions with the British Cabinet, Colonel House made it clear that this, and this only, was the kind of settlement that Wilson was prepared to use the House-Grey

Agreement to achieve. In other words, as House told the British leaders, the President would "throw the weight of the United States on the side of those wanting a just settlement—a settlement which would make another such war impossible."

Granted that Wilson's purpose was a genuinely neutral mediation, we can almost hear the critics say, how can one explain his seemingly provocative stand during the crises over armed merchantmen and the *Sussex*? Was he not making such a bold assertion of American rights in the hope that the German government would deny them and thereby give him an excuse for going to Congress for a declaration of war?

The answer, again, is that Wilson was trying desperately to prepare the way for peace and not for war. He and Lansing had proposed the disarming of merchant ships in the hope that this would facilitate a definitive understanding with Germany. But, as House and Page pointed out in urgent telegrams from London, such a proposal was unneutral in spirit and if implemented might mean the destruction of the British merchant marine; and Wilson's insistence upon it would assuredly disqualify him as a mediator acceptable to the Allies. Wilson suddenly reversed himself on the armed ship issue, therefore, primarily in order to restore his neutral standing. Then, following the conclusion of the House-Grey Agreement, the President pressed the Germans for guarantees of good behavior in the conduct of their submarine operations. But he did this with agonizing reluctance because of the risk of war involved and only in order to create a situation in which he might begin to move for peace.

All of Wilson's actions during the third and final stage in American neutrality, lasting from early May, 1916, to early February, 1917, confirm these conclusions. . . . Let us now see how he had meanwhile worked out his response to the continuing challenge of the submarine, and why.

So long as the British controlled the seas and the Germans commanded the strategic territories and resources of Europe, the American task of neutrality was the relatively easy one of accepting a *de facto* situation and of pursuing the most impartial policies possible within this framework of power. Thus Wilson permitted the German invasion of Belgium to pass without protest, even though some Americans contended that he was morally obliged to denounce such a gross violation of international law; thus he accepted the British maritime system. In this situation of actual stalemate, there was little likelihood of an Anglo-American rupture and no possibility of a German-American conflict, because there were no points of friction between the two governments. But the German decision to attempt to break the stalemate by using an untried weapon, the submarine, created a situation of great peril for the United States because it raised the issue of fundamental national rights and made it exceedingly difficult for the President to continue to steer a neutral course. Before we see how he struggled to find some adjustment to this new situation, let us consider for a moment some of the underlying factors that helped to govern German submarine policy and Wilson's response.

First, German decisions regarding the use of the submarine were determined almost exclusively by internal and objective considerations—the number of submarines on hand and their calculated effectiveness, the military situation in Europe and how it might be affected by American intervention, and the like—and in no essential way by American vis-à-vis the British, or by the rules of international law for cruiser warfare. Many historians have assumed that stern American resistance to the British maritime system, resulting in opening the channels of trade in noncontraband materials to the Central Powers, would have rendered the so-called submarine blockade unnecessary. This conclusion assumes that the Germans used the submarine only to force the British to abandon their own blockade. Actually, the chief and in the final showdown the only reason the Germans used the submarine was to cut Britain off from her indispensable sources of supply and thereby to win the war. To put the proposition in its strongest form, the Germans would have used the submarine to knock England out of the war when they had enough U-boats to accomplish this goal, even if the British had long since given up their maritime system altogether. That is to say, calculations of sheer military advantage or disadvantage and not American or even British maritime policies dictated the way in which the Germans would prosecute their underseas campaign.

Second, the submarine was in 1915 a new weapon of naval warfare. This was an important fact, for it meant that there was no special international law to govern its use when the rights of neutrals were involved. The only laws that could be applied were the rules of cruiser warfare, which required attacking warships to warn merchant ships before sinking them and to make provision for the safety of passengers and crew. The trouble was that the submarine was not a cruiser, but a frail craft that had to rely upon deception and quick striking power for safety and effectiveness. If its use had been an issue only between the belligerents, then international law would not have been much involved. But international law was directly involved, because its provisions defined not only the rights of neutrals, but their obligations to the belligerent powers as well. Having chosen a course of neutrality under international law, Wilson had to work within accepted rules in formulating his response to the submarine challenge insofar as American rights were concerned. The Allies, understandably, would not consent to modifications to permit enemy submarines to operate at their peak deadly efficiency; their refusal made it difficult for Wilson to insisit upon changing the rules without seeming to be unneutral in spirit and without in fact conferring enormous advantages upon the Germans.

Third, all questions of international law aside, a great power like the United States could not view the submarine blockade as a legitimate weapon, one that should be considered and perhaps accepted on grounds of expediency or necessity. This was true because at the time of its inauguration in February, 1915, the submarine blockade was actually a sham, since the Germans were then able to keep at most only seven U-boats at one time in all the waters surrounding the British Isles. The Germans, in fact, inaugurated the "blockade" with four submarines in service in the area. A year later, at the time of the *Sussex* crisis, the German Admiralty could send only eleven or twelve submarines into western waters at one time. Knowledge of these facts decisively influenced the way in which Wilson and his advisers viewed the so-called blockade and formulated policies regarding it, for it was one of the oldest and most generally recognized rules of international law that a blockade must be effective in order to be legal.

Fourth, unlike the Anglo-American disputes over trading rights, which involved only property interests, the German submarine campaign as it was often prosecuted raised an issue which no great power should ever evade or arbitrate—the safety and welfare of its people in pursuits and areas where they have a right to be. It is almost inconceivable that Wilson and the American people could have thought of going to war with the British over issues of search and seizure or of blockade. It is also inconceivable that they would not have been willing to think in terms of war with a government that permitted, indeed, instructed, its naval commanders to slaughter Americans indiscriminately upon the high seas.

It would, however, be a mistake of almost fatal magnitude to conclude, as so many writers have done, that Wilson's response to the submarine challenge was a simple and automatic reaction governed entirely by these factors. Although they played an important role, Wilson actually formed and executed, not a single consistent submarine policy, but a series of policies in response to changing issues and circumstances and in response to his own larger diplomatic objectives.

His first policy was formed in answer to the original German proclamation of submarine warfare. Avoiding the more difficult issue raised, the one involving the right of Americans to travel in safety on belligerent ships, Wilson replied by simply but strongly affirming the right of American vessels to use the seas subject to limitations permitted by international law, and by warning that the United States would hold Germany to a "strict accountability" (Counselor Lansing's words) for lives and property lost as a consequence of illegal submarine attacks against *American neutral* shipping. It was the only position that the President could have taken without abandoning the pretense of neutrality and national dignity, and the Germans soon retreated and gave such sweeping guarantees regarding American ships that this issue was never again a point of conflict between the two governments before 1917.

There still remained the necessity of devising a policy to deal with the more controversial issue of the right of American citizens to travel and work on *belligerent* merchant ships under conditions of safety specified by international law. When a German submarine sank the British liner *Falaba* without warning in March, 1915, killing an American citizen, Wilson's advisers in the State Department squared off in a momentous debate over the formulation of a proper response. One group, headed by Secretary Bryan, argued that American interests were not sufficiently involved to warrant a stern protest against submarine attacks on Allied ships, even when Americans were traveling on them, and that the spirit of neutrality demanded that the United States condone German violations of international law as it had done with British violations. The other group, headed by Counselor Lansing, replied that the attack on the *Falaba* had been such a flagrant infraction of international law that the United States must protest uncompromisingly in order to defend its neutrality and honor.

The records reveal that Wilson would have preferred to avoid any involvement while the two giant belligerents fought it out on the seas. In legal theory he agreed with Lansing, but he was so strongly moved by Bryan's pleading that he had apparently decided by the end of the debate over a *Falaba* note to make no protest at all. This is the course that he would probably have followed in the future if the Germans, by confining their underseas campaign to attacks against Allied cargo ships and by showing a desire to avoid the loss of American life, had made it possible for him to find a means of adjusting to the new situation.

A policy of noninvolvement, however, became impossible when a German U-boat sank the British passenger liner *Lusitania* without warning on May 7, 1915, with the loss of almost 1,200 civilians, including 128 Americans, men, women, and children. Wilson had to make some positive response now, so atrocious was the deed in the eyes of the American people, so flagrant was the violation of elemental national rights, so unneutral and degrading would be an acceptance of the terror campaign against the North Atlantic passenger liners.

The strategic facts of the situation—the German inability to maintain any effective blockade of the British Isles and the consequent serious dangers to Germany from a break with the United States—would have justified the President in peremptorily demanding prompt disavowal and guarantees. Wilson's response, however, reflected his own desire and that of the majority of Americans to preserve neutrality and to avoid taking any position short of yielding essential rights that might lead to hostilities with Germany. Thus all during the summer of 1915 Wilson pounded out notes on his typewriter, for the sole purpose of persuading the German government to disavow the sinking of the *Lusitania* and to abandon its campaign against unarmed passenger vessels. Threatening to break relations after a U-boat sank the liner *Arabic* on August 19, 1915, Wilson finally won the promise that he demanded.

By the end of the summer of 1915 the President had thus worked through two stages of policy and had won immunity from ruthless submarine attacks on American neutral ships and unarmed belligerent passenger liners. Up to this time, at any rate, Wilson had been patient, conciliatory, and firm only in his demand that the Germans give up measures that had already taken American lives and threatened untold others.

The third stage in the formulation of Wilson's policies toward the submarine, lasting from the early autumn of 1915 through the *Sussex* crisis in the spring of 1916, saw the President attempting to reach a definitive understanding with the Berlin authorities over all phases of submarine warfare against merchant shipping. The issue was daily becoming more difficult to solve by the application of traditional law, because the Allies since March, 1915, had been arming some passenger and cargo ships and ordering them to attack submarines that showed "hostile intent." But Wilson and Lansing persisted in trying to find a solution in spite of the obstacles because they (or Wilson, at any rate) and the majority of Americans still earnestly desired to avoid conflict over merely technical issues.

By patient negotiation Lansing finally won something resembling a German apology for the loss of American lives on the *Lusitania* and an implicit reaffirmation of the *Arabic* pledge. In order to hasten this German concession and to avert even the possibility of future contention, Lansing proposed his *modus vivendi* of January 18, 1916 (already mentioned), designed to provide a new code to govern the German underseas campaign against maritime commerce. This was the proposal that the Allies disarm their merchant ships and that the German submarines observe the rules of cruiser warfare in attacking them.

Adoption of the proposal by the opposing belligerents, or by the United States and Germany alone, would have achieved Wilson's objective of a comprehensive settlement of the submarine issue. And yet, for reasons that we have already seen, Wilson jettisoned the *modus vivendi* in order to save the House-Grey Agreement. Soon afterward, during the *Sussex* controversy (as we have also seen), he launched a new campaign to force the German government to conduct submarine operations against all merchant ships, armed and unarmed,[1] within the rules of cruiser warfare.

Wilson's rejection of the opportunity to come to a seemingly definitive understanding with Germany seems altogether logical and wise when we remember his objectives and the circumstances in which he made these decisions during the third stage in German-American relations. Wilson's supreme objective now was peace through his own mediation. Mediation seemed possible at this time only through the co-operation of the British government. But the British would co-operate only if they believed that the President was genuinely neutral, and certainly not if he insisted upon a code of submarine warfare that minimized the risks to Americans at the expense of British sea power to the advantage of an essentially illegitimate weapon.

Mediation was a noble objective with such great benefits to the United States that it justified taking a few risks to achieve. But Wilson could have followed no other course than the one he followed during the crises over armed merchantmen and the *Sussex,* even if his objective had been merely to maintain American neutrality. In the circumstances prevailing in the late winter of 1916, Wilson had to choose between continuing to accept the British maritime system, mooted by American Civil War precedents, or acquiescing in the challenge to that system, the German submarine blockade. The first was legitimate because it was based upon *de facto* power as well as legal precedent; the second was not legitimate because it was still a paper blockade without any power of effective enforcement. By insisting upon adherence to traditional rules insofar as the rights of Americans were concerned, Wilson was not at this time depriving the Germans of a weapon essential for their survival or one the free use of which would bring them victory at this time. This, essentially, was the reason that they yielded (for the time being) to Wilson's demands in the *Sussex* crisis.[2] By insisting upon the adoption of Lansing's *modus vivendi,* on the other hand, Wilson

---

[1] The author wishes to point out that this is a mistake, as the question of armed ships was not at issue in the *Sussex* negotiations.

[2] If the author were rewriting this lecture, he would emphasize the facts that Wilson and Lansing (by this time Secretary of State), while insisting upon the right of Americans to travel on armed merchantmen, also laid down such strict rules concerning *defensive* armament of merchantmen that submarines could (and often did) stop and sink armed ships without great danger to their own security; and that the German government was quite satisfied with the American position on armed ships. In any event, Wilson was prepared to accept unrestricted submarine attacks against armed merchantmen after it had become apparent, in early 1917, that the Allies were using armed merchantmen to attack submarines.

in effect would have changed the traditional rules and aimed a heavy blow at the British maritime system, and only for the illusory purpose of averting the possibility of a conflict with Germany.

The final test of any foreign policy is whether it serves the national interest. If it was to the interest of the United States to avoid participation in the war at any cost, regardless of its outcome, and if implementing the *modus vivendi* would have averted all possibility of American involvement, then Wilson's policies at this time were unwise. This generalization, however, is faulty in all its assumptions. To begin with, American interests would be best served by a stalemate and by a peace of reconciliation through Wilson's mediation, not by driving the Allies into sullen opposition, thereby making mediation impossible, and not by promoting a German victory. More important was the fact that implementing the *modus vivendi* would not have prevented the conflict with Germany that Wilson wished to avoid. As we now know, and as Wilson did not know, conflict would come inevitably when the Germans had enough submarines to institute an effective blockade. In that event neither right nor law nor concessions by the United States would dissuade the Germans from making an all-out bid for victory through a devastating attack upon all maritime commerce to the Allied nations.

With the conclusion of the *Sussex* crisis, Wilson's task of erecting a solid structure of neutral policies to govern relations with Britain and Germany was complete, and the next great effort of American foreign policy would be aimed at the higher goal of peace. Operating within the limitations imposed by American public opinion, external realities, and his own conception of the right role for the United States to play, Wilson had made the only kind of adjustments possible in view of American rights and duties as the leading neutral power. He was now in a position from which he could launch his peace campaign. Thus, by virtue of Wilson's leadership, American neutrality was not merely a fact in the spring of 1916, but the most important and the most hopeful fact of international life at the time.

There remains only the question whether it was wise. Some critics have argued that Wilson's great failure lay actually in being too neutral, in failing to see that conflict with Germany was inevitable, in failing to prepare the American people emotionally and physically to meet the test of war, and in failing to throw American resources and influence behind the Allies early in the war, in the same way that Franklin D. Roosevelt did in 1940 and 1941.

If one remembers the domestic circumstances and realities that helped to govern the formation of the policy of neutrality, and if one recalls that war with Germany did not *seem* inevitable at any time before 1917, then this criticism seems positively unreal. If one remembers Wilson's strenuous efforts to force a reluctant Congress to expand the nation's military and naval forces, and how he succeeded only partially because of popular opposition, then the criticism seems unfair. If one agrees that American interests, indeed, the interests of mankind, would have been best served by a peace based upon the inability of either side to impose sweeping terms, then the criticism seems also shallow.

Woodrow Wilson
and Collective Security: The Origins

EDWARD H. BUEHRIG

Edward H. Buehrig, a political scientist at Indiana University, was one of the first scholars to argue that considerable thought about long-range strategy and the vital interests of the United States underlay Wilson's responses to the diplomatic challenges raised by the war in Europe from 1914 to 1917. Professor Buehrig set forth these views in his provocative *Woodrow Wilson and the Balance of Power,* published by the Indiana University Press in 1955.

In the following selection, Professor Buehrig summarizes his views about the impact of the war on the United States and President Wilson. He then goes on to show how the ideal of a postwar collective security system germinated in the exchange of correspondence between the British and American governments in 1915. While this selection and the preceding one are not in conflict, they do demonstrate the way in which two scholars may differ in emphasis. Taken together, they show how varied were the threads in Wilsonian policy, which is so often simplistically described.

From Edward H. Buehrig (ed.), *Wilson's Foreign Policy in Perspective,* Bloomington: Indiana University Press, 1957, pp. 36–50. Reprinted by permission of the publisher.

THE FIRST WORLD WAR WAS SO SEVERE A CONVULSION OF WESTERN civilization, so shattering to the nineteenth-century pattern of world politics, that traditional American policy was bound to undergo important modification. What form the American reaction would in fact take was unpredictable. The range of possibilities was very wide, extending all the way from intensified isolation to the merging of national into international policy. Actually American policy was so severely shocked by the first World War that for two decades it lay immobile. Statesmanship, public opinion, and party politics, interplaying factors in a fluid situation, determined policy, or the lack of it, as we entered a new era of national existence. Of these it is my object to examine Wilson's statesmanship. By what path did he arrive at collective security? Why did he take this direction rather than some other? His goal having been determined, what of his tactics looking to its achievement?

When Wilson assumed the presidency, collective security was not a goal already formed in his mind, waiting for occasion to be born. The peace movement, so persuasive an influence of the time, undoubtedly conditioned Wilson's attitudes, as it had those of nearly all leading citizens of the Anglo-Saxon world. But Wilson had never associated himself with any of the numerous peace societies, nor indeed, on his own testimony, had he given any very systematic thought to international politics. Far from harboring ambitious schemes of reform, Wilson, an admiring student of Edmund Burke's writings, respected the force of habit in society and valued tradition for its stabilizing influence. In fact, it would appear that Wilson's zest for leadership derived not so much from devotion to a cause as from sheer love of the game, until in the League of Nations he embraced a cause that consumed him. It is not Wilson's biography, nor yet his personality, to which we must look in the first instance for explanation of his espousal of collective security, but rather to the circumstances of the war itself.

Wilson responded to the war by invoking neutrality. This was hardly a matter of choice, but an action dictated by the nation's past. Neutrality was the traditional American policy toward Europe, and had the war turned out to be of the nineteenth-century variety, neutrality would once again have been the appropriate reaction. But the whole of Europe was convulsed, and the war was, therefore, of more than local consequence. In two respects it touched the future prospects of the United States.

It threatened to bring a radical redistribution of power within Europe. Had Germany realized her ambition, which was directed not only against France and Russia, but against England as well, the United States would have had to make a hazardous adjustment to the new dispensation across the Atlantic. Since the New World, and notably the United States as its dominant member, had happily achieved accommodation with British power, the prospect of facing a new adjustment, with an ill-disposed Power, was doubly unattractive. That Wilson understood this possible consequence of the war cannot be doubted, for it is attested by numerous passages in his speeches. He did not suppose, speaking in January, 1916, that the United States need fear an invasion of its own territory. "What America has to fear, if it has anything to fear," he said, "are indirect, roundabout flank movements upon . . . the Western Hemisphere."

The second consequence of the European cataclysm was not so specific in terms of American interest, but no less ominous. It portended the decline of Western civilization. Indeed it hastened the end of the dominantly European phase of modern history. Henceforth the non-European world would rapidly emerge and assert itself against the European. In this looming confrontation all Europeans, including Americans (as we have ruefully come to realize in today's new postwar period), are in the same boat and we suffer as one from our self-inflicted wounds. This broad consequence of the first World War, not to be measured in terms of the relative advantage of European peoples among themselves, is plain in today's perspective; but it was perceived as well by many at the time, both here and in Europe. President Wilson and Colonel House felt most poignantly Europe's travail and were cognizant of its probable consequences. We have that most interesting comment of the President's at the Cabinet meeting of February 2, 1917. Relations with Germany were in crisis, but Wilson said that if, "in order to keep the white race or part of it strong to meet the yellow race—Japan, for instance, in alliance with Russia, dominating China—it was wise to do nothing, he would do nothing, and would submit to . . . any imputation of weakness or cowardice."

Concern for future security was not, however, the clear determinant of American policy toward the war and did not lead by a direct route to espousal of collective security. The tradition of aloofness was too strong. Mere counsels of prudence could not have overcome aversion to a deliberate intrusion on European politics. It is likely—and here we confront one of the imponderables of American history—that neutrality would have remained intact and a larger American policy unborn, had it not been for the serious difficulties that rose over the rules of maritime warfare. Freedom of the seas touches tangentially, and in a most curious way, on the emergence of collective security.

Consider the impact on world history of the German submarine, an innovation perfected only so brief a time before 1914, whose potency as a commerce destroyer was still unknown when the war began. It pushed American policy to the side of the Allies to a degree difficult to measure yet surely far-reaching in its consequences.

American neutrality, to be sure, was strongly inclined to the side of Great Britain even before the submarine entered the scene. This bias was the result of deeply rooted causes. Anglo-American accommodation in the New World—the product of a hundred years of negotiation and mutual forbearance—could not be lightly ignored by the American Government because Great Britain found herself in difficulties elsewhere. Moreover, there were immediate, tangible trade advantages to be derived from acquiescing in Britain's control of the seas and vast influence over the economic transactions of the world. Yet the injunction of impartiality contained in the law of neutrality in combination with Britain's desperate determination to wrest every possible advantage from her sea power would have raised a violent storm in Anglo-American relations had not the submarine provided a counter-irritant. And Anglo-American solidarity was, in turn, an indispensable condition to the emergence of collective security.

There was admittedly a strong element of hidden connivance in American policy. The law of neutrality did not oblige us to insist on the freedom of Americans to travel on belligerent vessels, nor did it, in view of the peculiar vulnerability of the submarine, dictate refusal to classify the armed merchantman as an offensive vessel. American policy was, in other words, not innocent of baiting the submarine. But whatever the alchemy of political motive, legal compulsion, and outraged opinion, the submarine was a potent factor bolstering benevolent neutrality and leading ultimately to American intervention in the war— thus furnishing quite inadvertently the springboard for a policy of collective security.

The public record of American relations with the belligerents was written in terms of freedom of the seas. Yet there was another strand of policy which employed a quite different criterion of American interest in the European disaster. Concerned only incidentally with episodes at sea, it took as the measure of policy the future security of the United States. As I have already suggested, there was awareness of the specific ways in which the United States might in the future be adversely affected. Still, the problem was not formulated narrowly in terms of American advantage, but broadly in terms of world stability. This aspect of American policy emerged publicly for the first time in Wilson's address on May 27, 1916, to the League to Enforce Peace.

Occupying a place in American history comparable to President Monroe's message to Congress of December, 1823, the address was a response to the circumstances of the twentieth century—as Monroe's message was a response to the circumstances of the nineteenth. And, as the Monroe Doctrine was the product of certain Anglo-American exchanges, so also was President Wilson's doctrine of collective security the result of an inner history involving Anglo-American diplomacy.

The story begins in the fall of 1914, and the initiative was that of Colonel House, who, with that purposeful energy so characteristic of him, sought through the belligerent ambassadors in Washington to promote a negotiated peace. Although these efforts were unavailing, they led by a circuitous route to Wilson's address of May 27, 1916.

Sir Edward Grey, the British Foreign Secretary, reacted to House's feelers of the fall of 1914 by raising the question whether the United States was prepared to become an active party to a European settlement. Grey perceived that Europe could no longer stabilize itself and that a passive role of good will on the part of the United States would fall short of meeting the situation. He seemed to favor a peace on the basis of German evacuation of Belgium and disarmament, but only if the United States would guarantee the settlement and, perforce, engage in an active European diplomacy. One cannot help admiring Grey's insight into the new requirements of world politics; and what he proposed was a veritable diplomatic revolution. It is reminiscent of Canning's calling in the New World to redress the balance of the old, but whereas Canning wished actually to seal off the New World to prevent its disturbing the balance of the old, Grey would summon the United States to an active role in Old World affairs. Such is the measure of the change wrought in international politics within a century's time.

In February, 1915, House met with Sir Edward Grey in London on the first of his wartime missions abroad for the purpose of seeking a negotiated peace. Grey urged that the United States throw its weight into the peace settlement, but House contended that to do so was impossible for it would be contrary to the fixed policy of the United States not to become involved in European affairs. Though it could not be party to the peace settlement, House declared that the United States would willingly join with other neutrals and the belligerents in a second convention dealing with rules of warfare. "In other words," House said, "it would merely be the assembling at The Hague and the adopting of rules governing the game."

To a less resourceful person than Grey this would have looked like a blank wall. House, however, in the course of elaborating on what he called "civilized warfare," had suggested establishing lanes of safety

99212

LIBRARY
COLBY-SAWYER COLLEGE
NEW LONDON, NH 03257

at sea in which the shipping of all countries, belligerent and neutral, would be immune from attack. The student of American diplomatic history will recognize in this a somewhat revised form of the traditional demand of the American Government for immunity from capture of non-contraband private property at sea. Sir Edward Grey now gave this historic American demand an ingenious twist. He suggested granting immunity from capture to all merchantmen, belligerent and neutral, regardless of location. This, however, on one condition: that all parties to the agreement go to war with any government violating that immunity. The upshot of such an agreement would be nothing less than collective security against aggression at sea.

Grey was trying to facilitate the transition of American policy from its historic preoccupation with freedom of the seas, that stereotype still so sharply etched in the first World War, to concern for the substance of international politics. Freedom of the seas would in the process be transformed; serving originally an economic purpose, it would under Grey's proposal serve a political purpose. Yet House, who keenly felt the need for somehow reconciling the old habits of American policy with the new requirements of international politics, seized upon the proposal as possibly offering a way out of his difficulties, took the idea to Berlin, and there advanced it as a basis for getting peace negotiations started—the first thread across the chasm, as he expressed it. In this, of course, he failed.

Subsequently Grey, having given the matter further thought, pointed out to House that Great Britain could not tie its hands at sea while German actions were unrestricted on land. Clearly then undertakings against aggression would have to apply on both land and sea. Thus Grey had come full circle. He had in these early soundings already used the term "league of nations" in referring to his proposed agreement for collective action against aggression.

After House returned to the United States in June, 1915, he received from Grey a series of letters urging the league idea. Writing on September 22, 1915, Grey became quite explicit:

How much are the United States prepared to do in this direction? Would the President propose that there should be a League of Nations binding themselves to side against any Power which broke a treaty; which broke certain rules of warfare on sea or land (such rules would, of course, have to be drawn up after this war); or which refused, in case of dispute, to adopt some other method of settlement than that of war?

This query resulted in much consultation between the President and Colonel House, and, after exchange of still further messages with Grey,

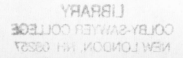
LIBRARY
COLBY-SAWYER COLLEGE
NEW LONDON, NH 03257

an answer was sent on November 10, 1915, declaring the intention of the United States to promote what Grey was advocating. Indeed a comparison of the points in Grey's letter of September 22 with what Wilson said in his subsequent address to the League to Enforce Peace shows how intimately connected was the emergence of the League of Nations with the inner workings of Anglo-American diplomacy. I shall presently quote the relevant passage. But first another observation about the May 27 address.

It must be remembered that a league of nations was being discussed in connection with the American desire for a negotiated peace. As originally envisaged by Wilson and House the purpose of the address to the League to Enforce Peace was not merely to announce American support of the idea of collective security but to call upon the belligerents to enter a peace conference. These two objects were related to each other; the proffered commitment of the United States to cooperate in the future suppression of aggression was meant an inducement to the belligerents to agree to "peace without victory." In fact, the address as originally projected was designed to implement the House-Grey memorandum of February 22, 1916. But Grey, despite insistent prodding by Colonel House, refused to give the word that the time to attempt negotiation had come. Wilson and House were thoroughly exasperated, but, unable to move Grey, they altered the character of the May 27 address on the eve of its delivery, abandoning for the time their plan to bring the belligerents to the conference table.

How far would Wilson commit the United States for the future? On this crucial point, so fraught with potential controversy, Wilson was already fairly explicit in his May 27 address. He saw a

universal association of the nations to maintain the inviolate security of the highway of the seas for the common and unhindered use of all the nations of the world, and to prevent any war begun either contrary to treaty covenants or without warning and full submission of the causes to the opinion of the world—a virtual guarantee of territorial integrity and political independence.

These are the very points, re-ordered and rephrased, that Grey had set forth the previous September. The statement is interesting in still another respect. The initial position accorded freedom of the seas and the emphatic manner in which this point is stated bespeaks Wilson's endeavor to tie his new policy to recognizable features of traditional American policy. This was not the last of many persistent efforts on his part to use freedom of the seas as such a connecting link. But logic in the end rebelled. Unless redefined out of all semblance to its historic meaning, freedom of the seas was incompatible with collective security. Finally at the Paris peace conference it dropped out of sight.

I call your attention also to the concluding phrase in the quoted excerpt from the May 27 address. The new policy would, Wilson said, amount to "a virtual guarantee of territorial integrity and political independence." We shall see that this formula had a special significance for Wilson, for it was another link between new and old policy—in this instance the Monroe Doctrine. Thus the effort was made as regards both leading principles of traditional American policy—freedom of the seas and the Monroe Doctrine—to establish continuity between past and future.

Wartime Anglo-American diplomacy was an important point of origin of collective security. Another beginning point, to which we now pass, was the Monroe Doctrine. To be sure, the Doctrine is a unilateral policy of the United States, concerned with any encroachment of non-American states on the western hemisphere. As such it does not constitute a system of collective security. What Wilson projected to the rest of the world, however, was a form of the Monroe Doctrine that had already undergone considerable modification. . . .

Wilson Moves to the Center of the Stage of World Affairs

ARTHUR S. LINK

Not the least important consequence of the War was the bold movement of Woodrow Wilson to the center of the stage of world affairs from 1916 to 1919. In the American President, liberals throughout the world found an eloquent spokesmen for their international ideals and an aggressive advocate of the new international order that they ardently desired to see established.

In the following extract from a lecture given over the British Broadcasting Corporation, the editor describes Wilson's peace move of 1916–1917—the first American thrust into European affairs—American entry into the war, and Wilson's rhetorical efforts to transform an imperialistic war into a great crusade for lasting peace through democratic collective security. This selection also shows some of the obstacles Wilson faced—abroad, at home, and even in the bosom of his official family—and leads one to wonder if his successive hopes were at any time near to attainment.

ALL THIS [THE SHOWDOWN WITH GERMANY DURING THE SUSSEX crisis] in Wilson's mind was mere prelude. The culmination would be an irresistible drive for peace through Anglo-American cooperation. Hence the President, using House as his intermediary, began

From Arthur S. Link, "Woodrow Wilson and Peace Moves," *The Listener*, LXXV (June 16, 1966), 869–871. Reprinted by permission of the British Broadcasting Corporation.

to apply heavy pressure on Grey to set the machinery of the House-Grey Memorandum in motion. Unfortunately for Wilson's hopes, Grey had never taken that memorandum seriously, any more than he had made any legal or moral commitments in its provisions. To the end of his tenure in the Foreign Office, he thought of American mediation under its terms as a last resort to be used only as an alternative to defeat, and never to be invoked so long as the Allies had any reasonable hope of military victory. Grey, in his refusal to consider American mediation, reflected the positions of all leading belligerents at this time. The French and Germans, still locked in a death grapple at Verdun, were in no mood for peace talks. The British were about to launch the great offensive on the Somme that they were sure would smash the German lines. Moreover, none of the belligerent leaders trusted Wilson. He was, they believed, unreliable, indecisive, and naive. Worse still, he seemed to face certain defeat in the Presidential election in November, 1916.

It was clear before summer had reached its midway mark that Grey would not cooperate. It was also clear that the American people were in no warlike mood. Neutralism and anti-war feeling surged through the country following the peaceful settlement of the *Sussex* crisis. It engulfed the Democratic Party, particularly, and made it possible for the President to make peace the leading issue of his campaign. American opinion had, moreover, turned sharply against the British on account of their intensification of the blockade and, more important, their severe suppression of the Easter Rebellion.

Wilson inevitably reacted to these upheavals in public opinion. But he was also undergoing profound changes in his own thinking about the war and his role as possible mediator. Grey's refusal to cooperate, along with other British actions, had convinced him that the Allies were fighting not for a just peace but to destroy Germany for selfish economic and military reasons. Hence, in his own mind, Anglo-American cooperation for peace through the House-Grey Memorandum was no longer desirable. His mediation, if the opportunity for it should come, would have to be an independent, truly neutral mediation.

That opportunity seemed to arrive in October, 1916, when the German government asked the President to move for peace and warned that it might have to resume unlimited submarine warfare if the President's efforts failed. Wilson was surprised but excited, and he at once began discussions about plans for independent mediation with his principal advisers on foreign policy, Colonel House and Secretary of State Robert Lansing. These discussions were protracted, bitter, and revealing. Lansing was by this time emotionally committed to the cause of the Allies.

He argued that American cooperation with Germany might well lead to a German-American sympathetic alliance if the Allies refused to come to the peace table. House supported Lansing, partly because he actually seems to have feared rupture and war with Britain.

Wilson rebuffed his advisers, saying that he was prepared to run these risks. But he could do nothing until the election was over. And even after his narrow reelection, he was diverted by domestic events and by certain German military measures in Belgium and several new submarine incidents. Meanwhile, the situation in Europe had changed, to Wilson's advantage and disadvantage. The Germans had invited Wilson's intervention in panic after Rumania's entry into the War, and while a strong Russian offensive in Galicia seemed to imperil the eastern front. By the end of November, the Germans and the Austro-Hungarians had not only turned back the Russians but had also virtually knocked Rumania out of the War. Even so, the German High Command believed that they would lose the War if they could not gain victory by 1917. They thought that their only hope of winning lay in an all-out submarine campaign. Not certain about its outcome, they permitted the Imperial German Chancellor, Bethmann Hollweg, to issue his own call for a peace conference on December 12.

The Allies were in an equally deep gloom on account of the failure of the Somme offensive and reverses in the east. A suggestion that the British should move at once for peace, made by Lord Lansdowne on November 13—not to be confused with Lansdowne's letter to *The Daily Telepgraph* a year later—set off a bitter debate in the Cabinet. Lloyd George, soon to become Prime Minister, believed that the War was lost. Worse still, from the British point of view, was the knowledge that the Allies were now so dependent upon the United States for munitions and supplies that the President held them in his hands.

To the President it was obvious that both the necessity and opportunity for his own independent action had come. He well knew that the Germans might launch a desperate submarine campaign, and that it might force the United States into the War. He also understood, at least partially, his absolute power over the Allies. Thus, still contrary to Lansing's advice, he launched his own peace bolt on December 18 by asking the belligerents to state the terms upon which they would be willing to end the War. This was the first public intervention in European affairs by a President since the founding of the United States. More important in our own context is the fact that it marked Wilson's emergence as a leading world figure.

Everything now depended upon the replies from Europe. The British and French leaders were stunned and outraged, but they well understood their helplessness and were in great disarray. Then Lansing intervened. Convinced that Wilson's course was disastrous, the Secretary of State set out to sabotage his peace effort. This Lansing did in several ways, but most importantly by intimating to the British and French Ambassadors that the Washington Administration expected their governments to say that their peace terms included, among other things, the return of Alsace-Lorraine to France, an indemnity for France, Belgium, and Serbia, and establishment of an autonomous Poland under Russian sovereignty. Lansing knew that an announcement of such terms would be tantamount to a second declaration of war and drive the Germans over the brink in submarine policy. And he almost certainly knew that the latter would lead to American military involvement.

Receipt of Lansing's advice in London and Paris on December 20, 21, and 22 dispelled all gloom and apprehension. An Anglo-French conference to frame replies both to Bethmann's and Wilson's peace bids opened in London on December 26. The conferees quickly agreed to announce precisely the terms that Lansing had suggested. The Germans, too, reacted exactly as the Secretary of State had anticipated. The Berlin government had earlier returned an evasive reply to Wilson because it wanted only his help in forcing the Allies to the peace table, not his participation in the conference. Publication of the Anglo-French replies convinced many German leaders that the war had to be fought to the finish and upset the precarious balance of power between the generals and admirals on the one side and the Imperial Chancellor on the other. An Imperial Conference at Pless, on January 9, approved the navy's demand for an all-out submarine campaign against all merchant shipping, including American ships, to be inaugurated on February 1, 1917.

Wilson, unaware of the full degree of Lansing's disloyalty, had been undisturbed by the Anglo-French replies. They were, he told the German government, pure bluff and not to be taken seriously. Nor was he discouraged by the German reply. His peace note of December 18 had been merely the first, public step. In mid-January he launched the second and decisive stage of his campaign—secret negotiations with the British and German governments with a view to his immediate mediation. While waiting for their replies, he went before the Senate on January 22 to tell the world what kind of settlement he had in mind and the American people would support. The peace to be made, Wilson said, had to be a peace of reconciliation—as he put it, "a peace without victory." "Victory," he went on, "would mean peace forced upon the loser, a victor's terms imposed upon the vanquished. It would be accepted in humiliation, under duress, at an intolerable sacrifice, and would leave a sting, a resentment, a bitter memory upon which terms of peace would rest, not permanently, but only as upon quicksand. Only a peace between equals can last." Moreover, the peace had to be built upon respect for self-determination for minority peoples and had to include measures for disarmament. The American people, he concluded, would be eager to join a league of nations to help enforce this kind of peace.

If Wilson's peace note of December 18 had made him a leading world figure for the first time, the "peace without victory" speech made him indubitably the commanding figure in the world. What Wilson did, in brief, was to marry the concept of a liberal settlement to the plan for a league of nations. By so doing, he at once became the hero, leader, and spokesman of the various liberal, labor, and socialistic groups throughout the Western world who had themselves long since worked out the program that the President now proposed.

It seemed for a moment that Wilson's bold stroke and secret negotiations might succeed. The British government, for reasons still unknown, returned a favorable response to Wilson's overtures on January 26. The Austro-Hungarian government soon sent secret feelers to the White House. Everything now depended upon the reply from Berlin. Bethmann was so excited by Wilson's secret appeal that he rushed to Pless to plead for a friendly response. It was too late to postpone the submarine campaign, for U-boats were already on the way to their stations. But the Imperial Chancellor did obtain permission to send a statement of moderate peace aims and an appeal to Wilson to persevere in his efforts for peace.

Events immediately afterwards led to an intensification rather than to an end to the war. But they need not have turned out that way. Wilson, to be sure, broke diplomatic relations with Germany on February 3, soon after the announcement of the new submarine campaign. But he was still as dead set against belligerency as ever. He clearly would have accepted a severe intensification of the submarine war, and he yielded to the growing American demand for war only after the Germans began to sink passenger liners and American merchantmen without warning, and only after the bungling Zimmermann telegram, proposing a military alliance between Mexico and Germany, had caused him to lose all faith in German good intentions. But in the end, when he made his final decision, it was the conviction that the War was in its last stages, and American participation would hasten its end, that most powerfully influenced the President to decide for belligerency.

Wilson's posture and policies inevitably changed somewhat after American entry on April 6, 1917. He did of course set full-scale mobilization on foot, and he was eager for Americans to do their share of the fighting as soon as possible. But his long-range objective—a peace of reconciliation—and his short-range goal—a negotiated peace as soon as possible—did not change, at least, not before the spring of 1918. Carefully disassociating himself from Allied war aims, he waited for some moves from Germany and Austria-Hungary to resume peace negotiations. He failed to respond to two such moves in the summer— adoption by the German Reichstag on July 19 of a resolution favoring a peace of reconciliation, and a peace appeal issued by Pope Benedict XV on August 1. But he was sorely tempted to respond more affirmatively than he did to the Pope's appeal, and was restrained only by warnings both at home and from the Allies that discussion of peace terms was premature. Wilson's eagerness to avow American peace aims in specific detail mounted all through the autumn of 1917. He did not miss the opportunity to speak out, once the Bolsheviks had seized power in Russia, published Allied secret treaties, and called upon workers and soldiers in the west to convert the War into a proletarian revolution.

Wilson went to work with the guidance of a group of young American liberals and experts whom House had assembled to make tentative plans for a peace settlement. The President embodied his program in his Fourteen Points Address to Congress of January 8, 1918. It was high time, he said, for peace-loving nations to avow their ideals and objectives. These Wilson proceeded to describe in a series of general points, including an end to secret diplomacy, freedom of the seas, general disarmament, the removal of artificial barriers to international trade, an impartial settlement of colonial claims, and establishment of a league of nations. Two points— the restoration of Belgium and self-determination for Russia—were, Wilson said, indispensable to a just settlement. Other points, including return of Alsace-Lorraine to France, an independent Poland with access to the sea, and autonomy for the subject peoples of the Austro-Hungarian Empire were desirable but presumably negotiable as Wilson said that they "should" rather than "must" be achieved. There was, finally, an implied fifteenth point—that the United States had no quarrel with the German people and no desire to continue the war for punitive or selfish ends.

It seems almost gratuitous to comment upon the significance of this address, so well known is it as the moral standard to which many peoples, including liberal Germans, rallied. But the Fourteen Points Address was much more than an avowal of peace aims. It was democracy's answer in its first full-dress debate with international communism. Lenin and Trotsky had appealed to the peace hunger of the world in order to begin a universal class war to destroy Western civilization in its democratic and Christian forms. In contrast, Wilson had appealed for peace in the name of all that was high and holy in the Christian democratic tradition in order to give Western civilization a second chance.

Wilson had also hoped to begin a dialogue with leaders of the Central Powers, and he did in fact succeed. But the discussion was cut short by the decision of the German High Command to risk everything upon one great final offensive to knock France out of the war before substantial American reinforcements could arrive. Ludendorff's great offensive of March, 1918, and the imposition by the Germans of the punitive Treaty of Brest-Litovsk upon the Russians in the same month, convinced Wilson that the war had to be fought to the bitter end, that, as he put it, only "righteous and triumphant Force" could make "Right the law of the world, and cast every selfish dominion down in the dust."

But even while he and his ever-growing armies waged war with increasing ferocity, Wilson refused to permit himself to be captured, much less enslaved, by the demons of total war. On the contrary, in the Four Additional Points of September 27, 1918, he made American peace aims even more explicit than ever before and continued to hope that a new German government would respond.

It is well known how the German government appealed to the American President in October 1918 for an armistice based upon Wilsonian terms and principles, and how Wilson through deft negotiation prepared the way for the armistice signed on November 11, 1918. Two facts about this momentous affair are, however, still not widely known. The first is that Wilson, by insisting on a negotiated peace, resisted a powerful movement, in his own country and among some of his own generals, for a march to Berlin. The second is that the President was eager to maintain sufficient German military power as a counterweight to French and British power once a conference had assembled. That, of course, it was not possible to do once the entire German Imperial structure collapsed unexpectedly in November.

Wilson had lost other trumps by the time that the Paris peace conference opened on January 18, 1919; but he was still the commanding figure in the world as he faced the great challenges of peace-making. By rhetoric rivaled in the modern era only by Churchill's, Wilson had given liberals and war-weary peoples everywhere hope for a new future based on justice and free from the terrors of war. He had forced the Allies (with certain reservations) as well as the Germans to agree to make peace upon a basis of liberal principles. The greater and more difficult task of converting hope into reality, and the greatest challenges to Wilson's leadership, now lay ahead.

The Flowering of Progressivism

ALLEN F. DAVIS

It would, of course, be a mistake to allow the diplomatic and military struggles of the years 1914–1918 to obscure the important changes that occurred within American society during the same period. In the following pioneering article, a historian of progressivism reveals the shallowness of the old interpretation that participation in World War I killed the domestic reform movement. Mr. Davis points out that, on the contrary, progressivism came to flower under the impact of the wartime experience.

O NLY A DECADE AGO HISTORIANS WERE SATISFIED WITH THE SIMPLE generalization that World War I killed the progressive movement, or that the crusade to make the world safe for democracy absorbed the reforming zeal of the progressive era and compounded the disillusionment that followed. "Participation in the war put an end to the Progressive movement," Richard Hofstadter announced. "Reform stopped dead," Eric Goldman decided. It is now obvious that the relationship between social reform and World War I is more complex. Henry May has demonstrated that some of the progressive idealism had cracked and begun to crumble even before 1917, while Arthur Link and Clarke Chambers have

From Allen F. Davis, "Welfare, Reform and World War I," *American Quarterly*, XIX (Fall, 1967), 516–533. Copyright, 1967, Trustees of the University of Pennsylvania. Reprinted by permission of the author. The footnotes in the original text have been omitted.

discovered that a great deal of progressivism survived into the 1920s. At the same time several historians have shown that for the intellectuals associated with the *New Republic* the war seemed something of a climax to the New Nationalism. And William Leuchtenburg has argued that the economic and social planning of World War I was a much more important model for the New Deal than anything that happened during the progressive era.

It is an overworked truism that there were many progressive movements, but one of the most important and interesting was the social justice movement. Led by social workers, ministers and intellectuals, the social justice movement, in broadest terms, sought to conserve human resources and to humanize the industrial city. The social justice reformers tried to improve housing, abolish child labor, limit the hours of work for both men and women, build parks and playgrounds and better schools. Like all progressives they believed that by altering the environment it was possible to reconstruct society. They combined optimism and a large amount of moral idealism with an exaggerated faith in statistics, efficiency and organization. Of course the social justice reformers did not always agree among themselves; prohibition, immigration restriction and the war itself caused divisions within the group.

The optimism and the idealism of the social justice reformers had been tempered before 1917. In a real sense the formation of the Progressive Party with its platform of industrial minimums had seemed the climax to their crusade. The collapse of the Progressive Party coming almost simultaneously with the outbreak of war in Europe led to shock and disillusionment and to many pronouncements that the war had ended social reform. The shock wore off quickly, though some of the disillusionment remained. Many reformers continued to promote social welfare legislation. They lobbied for the LaFollette Seaman's bill, and early in 1916 helped to force a reluctant Wilson into supporting a national child labor law. Most of the social justice reformers voted for Wilson in 1916 but without a great deal of enthusiasm. The specter of war hung over them as it hung over all Americans, but for many of them the acceptance or rejection of war was an especially difficult, and in some cases, a shattering experience. A few, like Jane Addams, Lillian Wald and Alice Hamilton, were consistent pacifists. Most of them opposed the preparedness movement and America's entry into the war, and they played important roles in organizations like the American Union Against Militarism. But when the United States declared war most of them went along with the decision, with fear and trembling but with loyalty. They feared that the crisis of war would cancel the victories they had won, that civil liberties would be abridged, that education and recreation and health standards would be neglected, that child labor and long hours for men and women would be resumed in the name of national need. Yet gradually, to their own surprise, many of them came to view the war, despite its horror and its dangers, as a climax and culmination of their movement for social justice in America.

Few of the reformers saw the war as a great crusade to make the world safe for democracy, at least in the beginning, but they were soon caught up in the feverish activity and enthusiasm for action that marked the first months of the war. Part of the excitement came from the thrill of being listened to after years of frustration, of plotting and planning and lobbying. "Enthusiasm for social service is epidemic . . . ," Edward T. Devine, the General Secretary of the New York Charity Organization Society, wrote in the summer of 1917, "a luxuriant crop of new agencies is springing up. We scurry back and forth to the national capital; we stock offices with typewriters and new letterheads; we telephone feverishly, regardless of expense, and resort to all the devices of efficient 'publicity work'. . . . It is all very exhilarating, stimulating, intoxicating." The reformers went to Washington; they also joined the Red Cross or the YMCA and went to France. For a time during the war the capital of American social work and philanthropy seemed to have been transferred from New York to Paris. Devine, who in 1918 was in Paris working for the Red Cross, wrote:

We have moved our offices to 12 Boissy d'Anglas, the Children's Bureau is on the ground floor; the Tuberculosis Bureau with the Rockefeller Foundation was already on the the third . . . , the rest of the Department of Civil Affairs is on the first floor, Bureau Chiefs and Associate Chiefs being marshalled along the street side in an imposing array, with Mr. [Homer] Folks and Mr. [John] Kingsbury at one end and Miss Curtis and myself at the other.

John Andrews, Secretary of the American Association for Labor Legislation, surveyed the new kind of administrator being employed by the government, many of them social workers and college professors, and decided that "Perhaps aggressive competition with Germany is having a beneficial effect on bureaucratic Washington." Andrews had gone to Washington in October 1917 to try to get the House to pass a bill, already approved by the Senate, providing workmen's compensation for longshoremen. With Congress ready to adjourn everyone assured him there was no chance for passage. But he went to see President Wilson, and the next day the bill passed the House under the unanimous consent rule. Andrews was amazed and found himself with a great stack of unused facts and statistics. "Usually before our bills are passed, we wear our facts threadbare," he remarked. "Perhaps this is not the most democratic way to secure urgently needed labor laws, but it is effective."

Not everyone of course shared the enthusiasm for war, nor the confidence that war would lead to great social gain. There was some truth in Randolph Bourne's charge that the intellectuals who saw so much good coming out of war were deceiving themselves and falling victim to the worst kind of chauvinism and rationalization. "It is almost demonical," Helena Dudley, a Boston settlement worker, wrote to Jane Addams, "the sweep toward conscription and these enormous war loans which Wall Street is eager to heap on: and labor so passive and the socialists broken up, and the social workers lining up with the bankers." Another woman reported from Seattle that there "the men who feel 'the call to arms' and the women who feel 'the call to knit' for the Red Cross are the men and women generally opposed to labor legislation and all progressive movements to increase the rights and well being of the many." But these were minority views.

Most of the social justice reformers joined John Dewey, Thorstein Veblen and the *New Republic* progressives and applauded the positive action of the Wilson administration in taking over the railroads, mobilizing industry and agriculture. They looked forward to sweeping economic reforms and contemplated the "social possibilities of war." "Laissez-faire is dead," one of them wrote, "Long live social control: social control, not only to enable us to meet the rigorous demands of the war, but also as a foundation for the peace and brotherhood that is to come." Some of them, inspired by the promise of the Russian Revolution and wartime socialism in England, looked forward to a kind of "democratic collectivism."

But the social justice reformers were concerned with more than an extension of the New Nationalism, and their primary interest was not in economic planning. They wanted to continue their crusade for social justice. Nothing was more important to them than the rights of the workingman, and the working woman and child. More than most progressives they had supported the cause of organized labor, and they were cheered by the rights won by labor during the war. The National War Labor Policies Board, the United States Employment Service and other wartime agencies recognized collective bargaining, the minimum wage and the eight-hour day, improved conditions of work and reduced the exploitation of women and children in industry. "One of the paradoxes of the war is the stimulus it is giving to human conservation," a writer in *The Survey* noted. The social justice reformers spent a large amount of time making sure labor standards were not weakened, and that women and children were not exploited during the war. Yet even the invalidation of the National Child Labor Law by the Supreme Court failed to dim their enthusiasm. The National Child Labor Committee set to work to design another and better law, and Congress responded by passing a bill that levied a 10 per cent tax on products produced by children under fourteen. A Supreme Court decision did not seem very important when Secretary of War Newton Baker and other members of the Wilson administration were saying publicly: "We cannot afford, when we are losing boys in France to lose children in the United States at the same time . . ., we cannot afford when this nation is having a drain upon the life of its young manhood . . ., to have the life of women workers of the United States depressed."

The crisis of war also stimulated the movement to improve urban housing. The housing movement was central to the social justice movement and intertwined with all other reforms from child labor legislation to progressive education. Much of the prewar movement, led by men like Lawrence Veiller, was devoted to passing restrictive legislation, but the war brought the first experiment with public housing. Borrowing something from the English example and spurred to action by the crucial need for housing war workers, the federal government, operating through the United States Shipping Board and the Department of Labor, built or controlled dozens of housing projects during the war. For many who had been working to improve urban housing for decades the government experiments seemed like the climax to the movement. Lawrence Veiller himself drew up the "Standards for Permanent Industrial Housing Developments" that were followed by the government agencies. The result was that the projects were much better designed and safer than those built by commercial builders. In addition the architects of the developments, influenced by the English Garden City Movement and by the settlement ideal of neighborhood unity, experimented with row houses, curved streets, recreation and shopping areas. Thus the public housing experiment of World War I was clearly the product of the city planning as well as of the housing movement of the progressive era.

The war also provided a climax to the social insurance movement, which had won very little support in the United States before 1910. Many states had passed workmen's compensation laws by 1917, but they were inadequate and filled with loopholes, and the philosophy of the movement was only gradually being accepted by many reformers, let alone the general public, when the United States became involved in World War I. Consequently the Military and Naval Insurance Act, which became law October 6, 1917, was hailed as a great victory by the leaders of the movement. The act, which was drawn up by Judge Julian Mack with the aid of experts like Lee Frankel and Julia Lathrop, required each enlisted man to make an allotment to his family, which the government supplemented. It also provided compensation in case of death or disability, and re-education in case of crippling injury. The architects of the plan hoped that it would prevent the demands for pensions and bonuses that had followed every American war, but more important to those who had fought for social insurance was the fact that the government had assumed the extra hazard involved in military service and guaranteed a minimum standard of subsistence to the soldier's family. The act was slow to get into operation, indeed some families did not receive their allotments until after the Armistice. It also put a heavy burden on the Red Cross, which tried to advance the money to needy families, but at the same time the act seemed to mark a victory for an important progressive measure.

Health insurance had made even less progress in the United States before 1917 than had workmen's compensation, but a group of social workers in 1915 picked it as the next great reform. "Health Insurance— the next step in social progress," became their slogan. A few states had amended their workmen's compensation laws to include industrial diseases, and New York, New Jersey, Massachusetts and a few other states were investigating the possibility of compulsory, contributory workmen's health insurance when the war came. The war seemed to increase the need. The New Jersey commission on old age insurance, in urging the government to enact a health insurance law, declared that "health protection . . . has been raised by the war from a position deserving of humanitarian consideration to one demanding action if we are to survive as a nation." But compulsory health insurance quickly aroused the opposition of the insurance companies and the medical profession, as well as of other groups who denounced it as "Prussianism." Not even the reminder that most of the British troops were protected by government health insurance could stop the opposition.

While health insurance fell victim to the war, or perhaps more accurately to a combination of circumstances, the movement to improve the nation's health was stimulated by the conflict. "War makes sanitation a common cause," Alice Hamilton announced. "We suddenly discovered that health is not a personal matter, but a social obligation," Owen Lovejoy remarked. Early fears that the war, by drawing doctors and nurses into the Army, would lead to a rise in infant mortality, tuberculosis, and other diseases proved groundless as a variety of agencies, volunteers and the federal government rallied to the cause. Lillian Wald, who opposed American participation in the war, served on the Red Cross Advisory Committee, traveled frequently to Washington as a consultant on health matters, and labored long and hard to keep the district nurses in New York functioning at top efficiency even during the influenza epidemic at the end of the war. Part of the stimulus to the health movement during the war came from the massive attempt to control venereal disease; part came from shock, especially over the rejection of 29 per cent of those drafted as physically unfit for service. But it was more than shock. As one social worker expressed it: "far from arresting public health progress, the war has suddenly defined America's public health problem. And the aroused public conscience has promptly enacted measures which a few months ago would have been tabled by leisurely officials and classed as visionary schemes. Into a year has been packed the progress of a decade."

Other reform movements seemed to make great strides during the war. The use of industrial education in rehabilitation work pleased the supporters of progressive education, while the mental hygiene movement approved the use of psychiatrists and psychiatric tests by the Army. The use of schools as community centers by the Council of National Defense led to the climax of the school social center movement, and the development of community councils and war chests stimulated community organization and led to acceptance of the federated fund drive.

Women also profited from the war. Out of necessity they achieved a measure of equal rights. They entered hundreds of occupations formerly barred to them, and their presence led to the establishment of the Women in Industry Service and ultimately to the Women's Bureau of the Department of Labor. "Wonderful as this hour is for democracy and labor— it is the first hour in history for the women of the world," Mrs. Raymond Robins, the President of the National Women's Trade Union League, announced in 1917. "This is the woman's age! At last after centuries of disabilities and discriminations, women are coming into the labor and festival of life on equal terms with men." The war also seemed to accelerate the movement for woman suffrage. Eight additional states gave women the vote, at least on some issues, during 1917. Wilson, after years of opposition, came out in favor of women voting, and the House of Representatives passed a woman suffrage amendment in January 1918.

The Negro and the immigrant often fell victim to racist hysteria during the war and did not gain as much as other groups. But the war seemed to hold hope even for the disadvantaged. Negroes were drafted and enlisted in the Army in great numbers and often served with distinction. All the training camps, recreation facilities and even the YMCA buildings were segregated, and there were many incidents of racial bitterness and a few of violence. Yet many of the social justice progressives, who had always been more sympathetic to the Negro's plight than had most reformers, hoped that the Negro's willingness to serve and what he learned in the Army would help lead to better conditions after the war. They were cheered by the appointment of Emmett J. Scott, Secretary of

Tuskegee Institute, as Special Assistant to the Secretary of War, and by the emergence of a number of young leaders within the Negro community. "We may expect to see the walls of prejudice gradually crumble before the onslaught of common sense and racial progress," a writer in *The Crisis* predicted.

It was hard to forget the bloody battle of East St. Louis and the race riot in Houston for which thirteen Negro soldiers were executed. It was easy to dwell on a thousand incidents of prejudice and on the lynchings that continued during the war, but many agreed with William E. B. DuBois when he called in July 1918 for the Negro to close ranks, support the war effort and put aside special grievances. "Since the war began we have won: Recognition of our citizenship in the draft; One thousand Negro officers; Special representation in the War and Labor Departments; Abolition of the color line in railway wages; Recognition as Red Cross Nurses; Overthrow of segregation ordinances; A strong word from the President against lynching. . . . Come fellow black men," DuBois urged his critics, "fight for your rights, but for god's sake have sense enough to know when you are getting what you fight for."

The war did not end the grievances, but it seemed to improve the Negro's lot. It also stimulated a massive migration. A large number of Negroes had moved north even before 1914 but the war and the lure of jobs increased the flow. Many Negroes did find employment, but they also encountered prejudice and hate. Social workers and a few other reformers continued to struggle against increasing odds to aid the Negro. Yet during the war the problems and the prejudice seemed less important than the promise for the future. The migration north and the large numbers who joined the Army also seemed to create improved wages and better treatment for Negroes in the South. The story of the migration might be told in terms of crime and corruption, of drift and hate, a writer in *Survey* noted but "Against it, there is a story of careful adjustment to new circumstances, of stimulation to self-help, of education . . . , of job findings and vocational guidance. . . ."

The story of the treatment of the immigrant and alien during the war was also not entirely bleak. German-Americans were attacked as radicals, pacifists and traitors, and wartime hysteria led to the development of superpatriotism and the decline of civil liberties. Yet at the time the patriotic enthusiasm seemed in some cases to accelerate the process of Americanization. The sight of many different ethnic groups joining enthusiastically to support Liberty Bond drives and other war activities led one observer to predict that the war would "weld the twenty-five or thirty races which compose our population into a strong, virile and intelligent people . . .," into "a splendid race of new Americans." The war also strengthened the movement to restrict immigration. In February 1917, a bill requiring a literacy test for the first time passed Congress and became law. There had always been disagreement among social justice progressives on the matter of restriction; some had argued that to help those already here it was necessary to reduce the flow, but the war seemed to end the debate. Not all reformers greeted the new law as a victory for progressivism, but no one, not even the Immigrant Protective League, launched an effective protest against the bill. The National Committee for Constructive Immigration Legislation, formed in 1918, and supported by a great variety of reformers, tried only to soften and define the restrictive legislation.

Despite occasional setbacks reform seemed to triumph in many areas during the war, but perhaps the most impressive victory came with the progressive take-over of the training camps. The Commission on Training Camp Activities was a product of the minds of Newton Baker and Raymond Fosdick. Baker, of course, had been a municipal reformer, and progressive mayor of Cleveland before becoming Secretary of War. Fosdick had been a settlement worker and Commissioner of Accounts in New York and an expert on American and European police systems. As Chairman of the Commission Fosdick picked men like Joseph Lee of the Playground Association, Lee Hanner of the Russell Sage Foundation and John Mott of the YMCA to serve with him. With the aid of several other private agencies the Commission on Training Camps set out to apply the techniques of social work, recreation and community organization to the problem of mobilizing, entertaining and protecting the American serviceman at home and abroad. They organized community singing and baseball, post exchanges and theaters, and even provided university extension courses for the troops. They moved out into the communities near the military bases and in effect tried to create a massive settlement house around each army camp. No army had seen anything like it before, but it provided something of a climax to the recreation and community organization movement and a victory for those who had been arguing for creative use of leisure time, even as it angered most of the career army men.

The Commission on Training Camp Activities also continued the progressive crusades against alcohol and prostitution. Clearly a part of the progressive movement, both crusades sought to preserve the nation's human resources, and were stimulated by a mixture of moral indignation and the latest medical knowledge. The prohibition movement had a long history, of course, but in its most recent upsurge it had been winning converts and legislative victories since the 1890s. The fight was led by the Anti-Saloon League and the Woman's Christian Temperance Union, but was supported by many social workers and social justice reformers who saw prohibition as a method of improving social conditions in the cities. But many of them had refused to go all the way with the crusade against alcohol. In New York a group of settlement workers had agitated against the Sunday closing of saloons; they appreciated that the saloon served as a social center. The most successful municipal reformers, including Newton Baker in Cleveland, carefully avoided enforcing some of the liquor laws, realizing how easy it was to antagonize the urban masses. The war stimulated the movement and brought it to a climax; it also ended the lingering doubts among many reformers. It became patriotic to support prohibition in order to save the grain for food, and for the first time in 1917 the National Conference of Social Work came out in favor of prohibition. But it was more than patriotism, for temperance was one key to social advance. Edward T. Devine announced after returning from Russia in 1917 that "the social revolution which followed the prohibition of vodka was more profoundly important and more likely to be permanent than the political revolution which abolished autocracy." Robert Woods, who had long supported prohibition, predicted in 1919 that the 18th amendment would reduce poverty, nearly wipe out prostitution and crime, improve labor organization and "substantially increase our national resources by setting free vast, suppressed human potentialities."

The progressive era also saw a major attack on prostitution, organized vice and the white slave trade, which seemed closely allied with the liquor traffic. Although the progressive vice reformer concentrated his attack on the madams and pimps and business interests which exploited the natural sex instincts of others, he also denied the time-honored defense of the prostitute, that it was necessary for the unmarried male to "sow his wild oats." Using the latest medical statistics, he argued that continence was the best defense against the spread of venereal disease.

Progressive attitudes toward alcohol and prostitution were written into sections twelve and thirteen of the Military Draft Act. They prohibited the sale of liquor to men in uniform and gave the President power to establish zones around all military camps where prostitution and alcohol would be outlawed. There was opposition from a few military commanders, a number of city officials and from at least one irate citizen who protested that red-light districts were "God-provided means for prevention of the violation of innocent girls, by men who are exercising their 'God-given passions.'" But Raymond Fosdick, with the full cooperation of the government, launched a major crusade to wipe out sin in the service; "Fit to Fight" became the motto. It was a typical progressive effort—a large amount of moral indignation combined with the use of the most scientific prophylaxis. Josephus Daniels, the Secretary of the Navy, disapproved of Fosdick's methods. He believed that urging the men to avoid sexual contact was the best and only way to reduce disease; "Men must live straight if they would shoot straight," he told the sailors on one occasion. But when the disease rate in the Navy became the highest in the service he gave in to Fosdick's demand that science as well as moralism be used. The crusade was successful, for by the end of 1918 every major red-light district in the country had been closed, and the venereal disease rate had been lowered to produce what one man called, "the cleanest Army since Cromwell's day."

To protect the health of the soldiers was not enough, however; "We must make these men stronger in every sense, more fit, morally, mentally and physically than they have ever been in their lives . . . ," one recreation worker announced. "These camps are national universities—training schools to which the flower of American youth is being sent." When the boys go to France, "I want them to have invisible armour to take with them," Newton Baker told a conference on War Camp Community Service. "I want them to have armour made up of a set of social habits replacing those of their homes and communities."

France provided a real test for the "invisible armour" of the American soldier. He was forbidden to buy or to accept as gifts any alcoholic beverage except light wine and beer. Despite hundreds of letters of protest from American mothers, Fosdick and Baker decided it would be impossible to prevent the soldiers from drinking wine in France. But sex posed a more serious threat, for both the British and French armies had tried to solve the problem of venereal disease by licensing and inspecting prostitutes. Clemenceau could not understand the American attempt to outlaw prostitution and even accused the American Army of spreading disease among the French civilian population. He graciously offered to provide the Americans with licensed prostitutes. General Pershing considered the offer "too hot to handle" and gave it to Fosdick. When Fosdick showed it to Baker, the Secretary of War remarked, "For God's sake, Raymond, don't show this to the President or he'll stop the war." The Americans never accepted Clemenceau's invitation and he continued to be baffled by the American progressive mind.

One of the overriding assumptions of those who sought to protect the American soldier at home and abroad was that he would learn from his experience and return to help make a better America after the war. Indeed one of the major reasons for the optimism of the social justice reformers was their confidence that the experiments and social action of the war years would lead to even greater accomplishments in the reconstruction decade ahead. Robert Woods surveyed the positive actions of the federal government during wartime in the spring of 1918 and asked, "Why should it not always be so? Why not continue in the years of peace this close, vast, wholesome organism of service, of fellowship, of constructive creative power?" Even Jane Addams, who saw much less that was constructive about war than did many of her colleagues, lectured for Herbert Hoover's Food Administration, and looked ahead with confidence and hope for the future. Paul Kellogg, editor of *The Survey*, also mirrored some of the hope for continuing the reform that the war had accelerated when he wrote to his subscribers in September 1918:

> With hundreds of people for the first time shaken out of their narrow round of family and business interests and responding to public service as a patriotic call, with American help going out to the far ends of the earth as at no time since the early stages of the missionary movement; with federal action affecting housing, labor relations, community life, as never before; with reconstruction plans afoot in England and France . . . we feel that *The Survey* has never before faced such a great obligation and such a great opportunity.

Of course the enthusiasm for the present and optimism for the future was sometimes tempered by doubts. There was the occasional glimpse of the horror of war, especially by those who went overseas. There was the abridgment of the freedom of speech and the persecution of radicals and aliens and pacifists. There was the fear that opposition or apathy would arise after the war to strike down the gains, and that the American labor movement, led by Gompers, was too conservative to take advantage of the opportunity for labor advance. There was even a lingering worry about the very enthusiasm for reform that made the war years exciting, concern over the disappearance of the opposition and even the decline of debate over immigration restriction, prohibition and other measures. But the doubts were few and far between. Most of the social justice reformers surveyed the success of social reform at home and looked confidently toward the future. For them the war was not so much a war to make the world safe for democracy as it was a war that brought to a climax their crusade for reform at home.

Yet the progressives deluded themselves. They were the victims of their own confidence and enthusiasm, for the social reforms of the war years were caused more by the emergency situation than by a reform consensus. Quickly after the war, the Wilson administration abandoned public housing and social insurance, and withdrew the government from positive participation in many areas. The gains for labor and the Negro proved ephemeral, and the dream that the newly enfranchised women, together with a generation of young men educated on the battlefields and in the training camps, would lead a great crusade to reconstruct America turned out to be idealistic in the extreme.

By 1920 there was little left from wartime social reform except prohibition, immigration restriction and racist hysteria. The disillusionment
that followed can be explained in part by the false hopes raised by the
war. Many social justice progressives had been discouraged by the failure
of the Progressive Party, then rescued by the excitement of the wartime
social experiments. The collapse of the dreams fostered by the war
changed American reformers irrevocably. They would never again be
quite as optimistic and enthusiastic. Their faith in statistics and their
confidence that the American people really wanted reform were shat-
tered. Yet the despair was not complete—it never reached the depths that
marked the group of young intellectuals which Ernest Hemingway came
to symbolize. Their disillusionment was tempered by a lingering vision
of social justice, a vision of government action to protect the rights of
labor, and especially the working woman and child, of public housing
and social insurance, of equal opportunity for the Negro and other
minorities.

A number of social justice progressives worked quietly and sometimes
forlornly during the twenties preparing to battle for the success of some
of their plans in the 1930s and after. Very often their point of reference
was World War I. It is no longer possible to say simply that the war
ended the progressive movement. It was not the war itself which killed
reform, but rather the rejection afterward of the wartime measures which
seemed at the time to constitute the climax to the crusade for social
justice. Yet scholars interested in the collapse and survival of progressivism should examine the war years, for here were raised some of the
hopes that were later dashed and some of the dreams that were later
fulfilled.

The Impact of the War on the American Political Economy

WILLIAM E. LEUCHTENBURG

With insight gained from an intimate knowledge of the New Deal era, William E. Leuchtenburg of Columbia University in the following article has greatly enriched both our knowledge of the American mobilization effort of 1917–1918 and our understanding of the long-term significance of that effort. As Mr. Leuchtenburg points out, despite the efforts of prewar Progressives, there had been remarkably little governmental intervention in the national economy before 1917. The War brought a dramatically new elaboration of governmental controls, which guided New Dealers in battling a domestic enemy, fifteen years later.

Once again, the different emphases of two historians deepens our understanding of the events they describe. In the preceding selection, writing of the war as a culmination, Mr. Davis stresses the reforms that flowed from men and agencies outside the federal government. Mr. Leuchtenburg, who approaches the War as a starting point, focuses on centralized power.

From William E. Leuchtenburg, "The New Deal and the Analogue of War" in *Change and Continuity in Twentieth-Century America*, John Braeman, *et al.* (eds.), pp. 84–88, 90–107, 109–113, 117–120, 122–125, 142–143. Copyright © 1964 by the Ohio State University Press. Most of the footnotes in the original text have been omitted.

IN TRACING THE GENEALOGY OF THE NEW DEAL, HISTORIANS HAVE paid little attention to the mobilization of World War I. Instead, they have centered their interest on two movements: populism and progressivism. Both were important antecedents—a reasonably straight line may be drawn from the Populist sub-treasury plan to the Commodity Credit Corporation, from the Pujo committee to the Securities and Exchange Commission. Yet in concentrating on populism and progressivism, writers have given too little attention to the influence of the wartime mobilization, which may have been as great as the example of the Progressive era and certainly was more important than populism.

• • •

World War I marked a bold new departure. It occasioned the abandonment of laissez faire precepts and raised the federal government to director, even dictator, of the economy. The War Industries Board mobilized production; the War Trade Board licensed imports and exports; the Capital Issues Committee regulated investment; the War Finance Corporation lent funds to munitions industries; the Railroad Administration unified the nation's railways; the Fuel Administration fixed the price of coal and imposed "coal holidays" on eastern industry; and the Food Administration controlled the production and consumption of food. The Lever Food and Fuel Control Act of 1917 gave the President sweeping powers: to take over factories and operate them, to fix a maximum price for wheat, and to license businesses in necessaries. By a generous interpretation of its powers, the War Industries Board supervised pricing, compelled corporations to accept government priorities, and forced companies to obey federal edicts on how to dispose of their products. "This is a crisis," a War Industries Board representative scolded steel-industry leaders, "and commercialism, gentlemen, must be absolutely sidetracked." Actions of this character, as well as the proliferation of public corporations ranging from the United States Housing Corporation to the Spruce Production Corporation, proved important precedents for New Deal enterprises fifteen years later.

The field of labor relations may serve as a single example of the difference in importance of the Populist and Progressive experience and that of World War I. Prior to the war, no serious attempt had ever been made to empower the federal government to uphold the right of collective bargaining. Federal action was limited to peripheral areas. When class lines were drawn in labor disputes, Progressives frequently aligned themselves against the unions. But in World War I, the War Labor Board proclaimed its support of union rights and, to the discomfiture of businessmen, enforced these rights. Many of the labor policies pursued in the war months would have been inconceivable a short while before. When the Smith & Wesson Arms Company of Springfield, Massachusetts, insisted on its prerogative to require workers to sign yellow-dog contracts, the War Department commandeered the plant, even though the Supreme Court had upheld the legality of such contracts. The government even dared to seize Western Union when the president of the firm denied his employees the right to join the Commercial Telegraphers Union. The panoply of procedures developed by the War Labor Board and the War Labor Policies Board provided the basis in later years for a series of enactments culminating in the Wagner National Labor Relations Act of 1935.

The war gave a home to the new class of university-trained intellectuals which had emerged in the generation before the war. While some of them had found a career in public service in state governments before 1917, few had worked in the national government, chiefly because there was so little in Washington for them to do. After the United States intervened, Washington swarmed with professors, until, one writer noted, "the Cosmos Club was little better than a faculty meeting of all the universities." In all countries, he observed, professors "fought, and they managed affairs, thus refuting the ancient libellous assumption that they constituted an absent-minded third sex. . . ."

Public administrators of this type represented a new force in American politics. They were advisers and technicians but, more than that, men of influence and even of power. At a time when class conflicts were sharpening, they did not reflect particular classes so much as the thrust for power of *novi homines* who had a significant role to play on the national stage. Some like Gifford Pinchot had made their appearance in Washington before the war, and still more like Charles McCarthy had been active in such reform capitals as Madison and Albany, but it was the war which offered them an unparalleled opportunity. Randolph Bourne noted perceptively the "peculiar congeniality between the war and these men. It is as if the war and they had been waiting for each other." Phenomena almost wholly of the twentieth century, they came by the 1930's to have a crucial part in shaping legislation and in manning the new agencies which their legislation developed. The passage of the Wagner Act in 1935, for example, resulted less from such traditional elements as presidential initiative or the play of "social forces" than from the conjunction of university-trained administrators like Lloyd Garrison within the New Deal bureaucracy with their counterparts on senatorial staffs like Leon Keyserling in Senator Wagner's office.

•   •   •

The end of the war left the administrators with a sense of incompletion. One writer noted unmistakable shadows of annoyance at the Cosmos Club when "the dark cloud of peace" lowered in October, 1918. After the war, to the chagrin of the planners, the economic machinery was quickly dismantled, but the lesson that the war had taught—that the federal government could mobilize the nation's resources in a planned economy—was not forgotten. Throughout the 1920's, the more advanced Progressives looked back fondly toward the war mobilization which seemed to have drawn a blueprint for America's future. In 1927, Rexford Tugwell lauded the war as "an industrial engineer's Utopia." He wanted to coordinate the economy as it had been under the War Industries Board in "America's war-time socialism." "We were on the verge of having an international industrial machine when peace broke," he wrote ruefully. ". . . Only the Armistice," he lamented, "prevented a great experiment in control of production, control of price, and control of consumption."

The fascination the war example held for the Progressives was a consequence of the fusion of nationalism and reform in the previous generation. Heralded by Bismarck in Germany and Joseph Chamberlain in Great Britain, this conjunction appeared in America in the martial fantasies of Edward Bellamy, in Francis Walker's critique of classical economics, in the "industrial armies" of men like Jacob Coxey, in the military forms of the Salvation Army, and in the response of certain reformers to the imperialist issues of the 1890's.[1] In the Progressive era, this association was starkly revealed in the career of Theodore Roosevelt who thought social justice and military preparedness to be two aspects of a common program.

While the confluence of nationalism and reform fascinated a number of progressive theorists, notably Brooks Adams, it was Herbert Croly who, in his seminal *The Promise of American Life,* explored the relationship most extensively. Croly set down the deep dissatisfaction of the Progressives with the quality of life in America. The homogeneity of the early republic, he wrote, had been fragmented by a century of individualism

---

[1] In some respects, this relationship had even earlier antecedents, for example, in the special place that Lincoln and the Union cause had in the hearts of post-bellum reformers. It might even be traced back as far as the congruence of reform and imperialism in the Jefferson administration.

run riot. So long as the market place determined values, so long as each individual or interest was permitted to pursue its own ends with no commitment to a common ideal, the result could not help but be unsatisfying, Croly reasoned. Reform had foundered because it lacked a sense of national purpose. "In this country," he observed, "the solution of the social problem demands the substitution of a conscious social ideal for the earlier instinctive homogeneity of the American nation."

The war offered just such a "conscious social ideal." Through war priorities, as Bernard Baruch later explained, the economy could be "made to move in response to a national purpose rather than in response to the wills of those who had money to buy." The nationalistic demands of war denied, if only for a time, the claims of the profit system. ". . . When production and distribution became really a matter of life and death, immediate and dramatic, every warring nation, after a few months of appalling waste, threw laissez-faire out of the window," noted Stuart Chase. "Wars must be won, and it was painfully obvious that laissez-faire was no help in winning them." The individualistic, competitive economy of the prewar years had to submit to the discipline of conscious government direction. Not business profit but the national interest was to determine how resources were to be allocated. The old system of competition, Rexford Tugwell wrote jubilantly, "melted away in the fierce new heat of nationalistic vision."

When the stock market crash of 1929 precipitated the Great Depression of the 1930's, Progressives turned instinctively to the war mobilization as a design for recovery. The War Industries Board, Stuart Chase pointed out, had, like the Soviet *Gosplan,* demonstrated that "super-management" could replace "industrial anarchy." . . . Such men as Gerard Swope of General Electric, a veteran of the war mobilization, and Otto T. Mallery, the leading advocate of public works in the World War I era, recommended floating large federal bond issues like Liberty Bonds to finance a massive public-works program. . . . The Wisconsin economist Richard T. Ely went a step farther. He proposed the creation of a peacetime army which, when a depression struck, could be expanded by recruiting from the ranks of the unemployed. Under the direction of an economic general staff, the army, Ely urged, "should go to work to relieve distress with all the vigor and resources of brain and brawn that we employed in the World War."

By the middle of 1931, both businessmen and politicians were calling on President Hoover to adopt the procedures of the War Industries Board to pull the country out of the depression. When William McAdoo, who had headed the wartime Railroad Administration, proposed a Peace Industries Board in June, 1931, he found ready support. The War Industries Board, one correspondent wrote McAdoo, "accomplished wonders during the war, and there is no question but that a board established now to coordinate things in our national industries will also do wonders. This historical precedent is a great asset and ought to guide us in our national planning for the benefit of all." A month later, Charles Beard urged the creation of a National Economic Council with a Board of Strategy and Planning which would follow the pattern of "the War Industries Board and other federal agencies created during the titanic effort to mobilize men and materials for the World War." The following month, Representative Chester Bolton of Ohio advanced a similar proposal. "If we could have another body like the old War Industries Board," he wrote the head of Hoover's voluntary relief agency, "I believe the situation today could be greatly bettered." In September, 1931, Gerard Swope came forth with the most influential of all the pre-New Deal proposals: the "Swope Plan" to stabilize employment and prices through a constellation of trade associations under a national economic council. Early in 1932, a group of more than a hundred businessmen requested Hoover to declare a two-year truce on destructive competition and urged him "to consider a return to war-time experience by bringing into existence A National Economic Truce Board."

The cornucopia of proposals included suggestions with widely differing ideological implications. Some called on the war example to support radical recommendations for national planning; others used the war precedent simply as a stratagem to free business of the encumbrance of the trust laws. Most of them had in common a demand for greater initiative by the federal government, and many of them—especially the public-works proposals—called for a sharp increase in government spending.

Such proposals ran far ahead of anything President Hoover and his followers would countenance. Most businessmen seemed chary of taking the War Industries Board as a model for peacetime. The President himself gave little indication of a readiness to have the federal government assume a larger role. To be sure, he signed an Employment Stabilization Bill in 1931, and gave a major share of credit for the measure to Mallery. But he deplored recommendations for lavish federal spending. Ventures of this sort, the President protested, would unbalance the budget and destroy business confidence in public credit.

These doctrines received small credence from men who recalled the war expenditures. "If it is permissible for government to expend billions in wartime in the organization of production, it is no less legitimate for government in a great emergency of peacetime to do what it is also impossible for private individuals to accomplish," reasoned the distinguished economist Edwin R. A. Seligman. The popular economic writer William Trufant Foster scolded:

If any one still doubts that our economic troubles are mainly mental, let him consider what would happen if the United States declared war today. Everybody knows what would happen. Congress would immediately stop this interminable talk and appropriate three billion dollars—five billion—ten billion—any necessary amount. . . .

Some day we shall realize that if money is available for a blood-and-bullets war, just as much money is available for a food-and-famine war. We shall see that if it is fitting to use collective action on a large scale to kill men abroad, it is fitting to use collective action on an equally large scale to save men at home.

•   •   •

President Hoover made much more forceful use of the war precedent to meet the financial crisis of the autumn of 1931. In December, 1931, Hoover asked Congress to create a Reconstruction Finance Corporation frankly modeled on the War Finance Corporation. The proposal appeared to originate at about the same time in the minds of several different men: Hoover, Federal Reserve Governor Eugene Meyer, who had been managing director of the WFC, Louis Wehle, who had been the WFC's general counsel, and Senator Joseph Robinson of Arkansas. All drew their inspiration from the WFC. "The RFC was a revival of the War Finance Corporation, that's all, but with expanded powers," Meyer recalled. Observers were astonished by the speed with which Congress approved the RFC bill. "It puts us financially on a war basis," noted the *New Republic*. When the RFC began operations, it employed many of the WFC's old staff, followed its pattern and that of the wartime Treasury in financing, and even took over, with slight modifications, the old WFC forms for loan applications.

•   •   •

New York's Governor Franklin D. Roosevelt sought to reap political advantage from these different perceptions of the war experience. In his campaign for the Democratic Presidential nomination in 1932, Roosevelt contrasted Hoover's performance with the achievements of the war mobilization. In his "forgotten man" address in Albany on April 7, 1932, Roosevelt declared that American success in the war had been due to leadership which was not satisfied with "the timorous and futile gesture" of sending a small army and navy overseas, but which "conceived of a whole Nation mobilized for war, economic, industrial, social and military resources gathered into a vast unit." The United States in 1932, Roosevelt asserted, faced "a more grave emergency than in 1917," and in meeting that emergency the Hoover administration had neglected "the infantry of our economic army." "These unhappy times," the Governor observed, "call for the building of plans that rest upon the forgotten, the unorganized but the indispensable units of economic power, for plans like those of 1917 that build from the bottom up and not from the top down, that put their faith once more in the forgotten man at the bottom of the economic pyramid." Less than two weeks later, at the Jefferson Day Dinner at St. Paul on April 18, Roosevelt repeated that the nation faced an emergency "more grave than that of war" and once more derided Hoover's efforts to meet the crisis. He added pointedly:

Compare this panic-stricken policy of delay and improvisation with that devised to meet the emergency of war fifteen years ago.

We met specific situations with considered, relevant measures of constructive value. There were the War Industries Board, the Food and Fuel Administration, the War Trade Board, the Shipping Board and many others.

The 1932 election brought the Democrats to power for the first time since Wilson's war administration. It was "only natural," as [Carl B.] Swisher has observed, "that some of the World-War leaders should return to federal office and that others should become unofficial advisers of the administration. They, like the President, thought in terms of the dramatic concentration of power in the federal government which they had helped to bring about for the defeat of a foreign enemy. It is not surprising that modes of procedure were carried over from one period to the other." In the interregnum between Roosevelt's election in November, 1932, and his inauguration in March, 1933, war recollections became even more compelling. The whole political system seemed doomed to self-asphyxiation. The discords of party, the deadlock in Congress, the maxims of the classical economists, the taboos of the Constitution all seemed to inhibit action at a time when action was desperately needed. In contrast, the war was remembered as a time of movement and accomplishment.

During the interregnum, the country debated a series of new proposals for utilizing the war experience to vanquish the depression. Daniel Roper, who would soon be Roosevelt's Secretary of Commerce, suggested a few days after the election that the new President "appoint one 'super' secretary with the other secretaries assistant to him and organize under this 'super' secretary the plan of the National Council of Defense composed of, say 21 men working without compensation as they did in

War times." Many believed the crisis could be met only by vesting in the President the same arbitrary war powers that Woodrow Wilson had been given.

• • •

As early as the spring of 1932, weeks before Roosevelt had even been nominated, his brain trust had requested Joseph D. McGoldrick and Howard L. McBain to prepare a memorandum on Presidential war powers, for they anticipated Roosevelt would need them as authority for emergency acts. Early in January, 1933, the President-elect asked Rexford Tugwell to explore the possibility that the Trading with the Enemy Act of 1917 might provide the basis for an edict embargoing gold exports. Tugwell's research quickly involved him in a comedy of errors in which the New Dealers sought both to obtain the necessary information without letting the Hoover Administration learn what they were up to and at the same time to persuade themselves that a statute that had been amended many times gave them the legal authority to do what they intended to do anyway. Governor Roosevelt's legal aides could not have been more co-operative. Senator Thomas Walsh, Roosevelt's choice to be Attorney General, promised that, if the President-elect found he needed the powers, he would quiet his doubts and rule that the old statute gave him the authority he required. When, after Walsh's death, Roosevelt picked Homer Cummings for the post, he turned over to him the folder on the Trading with the Enemy Act. Cummings obligingly found the statute was still alive.

As the day of Roosevelt's inauguration approached, the epidemic of bank failures drove governors in state after state to proclaim bank holidays and raised fears that the economic system was on the verge of collapse. "A blight has fallen over all American industry," declared the Akron *Beacon-Journal* on March 3. "A foreign invader making easy conquest of our shores could do no worse." As Roosevelt took the oath of office, the atmosphere in Washington, wrote Arthur Krock, was like that "in a beleaguered capital in war time."

Roosevelt's inaugural address on March 4, 1933 reflected the sense of wartime crisis. The nation, he resolved, must move "as a trained and loyal army willing to sacrifice for the good of a common discipline." He would ask Congress to adopt his legislative program, but if Congress failed to act and the emergency continued, the new President announced: "I shall not evade the clear course of duty that will then confront me. I shall ask the Congress for the one remaining instrument to meet the crisis—broad executive power to wage a war against the emergency, as great as the power that would be given to me if we were in fact invaded by a foreign foe."

During the "Hundred Days," President Roosevelt sought to restore national confidence by evoking the mood of wartime: the feeling of national unity above any claim of partisan or private economic interest because the very existence of the country was imperiled. The opposition press suspended criticism of the President; business corporations, labor unions, and farm organizations pledged their cooperation; and Republican leaders urged the country to rally around the Democratic chief executive. Governor Landon declared: "If there is any way in which a member of that species, thought to be extinct, a Republican Governor of a midwestern state, can aid [the President] in the fight, I now enlist for the duration of the war."

The New Deal hoped to arouse the same sense of devotion to the nation and the same spirit of sacrifice that had been displayed in the war. "It is important," wrote Rexford Tugwell, "that we should again explore the possibilities of what William James called 'the moral equivalents' of war." "The ordeal of war," he told Dartmouth students, "brings out the magnificent resources of youth. . . . The ordeal of depression ought to try your mettle in similar ways. . . . The feeling which shook humanity during the War and which after the War reshaped the entire civilization of mighty nations is called for again."

When the planners of the thirties looked back at the war, they were most impressed by how much had been accomplished once the nation had been unified by allegiance to a common purpose. Writers like Rexford Tugwell and George Soule argued that the effective functioning of "a regime of industrial democracy" required the same spirit of "loyalty to larger aims" that the War Industries Board had exploited. Nationalistic to the core, unabashedly patriotic, they believed that if the country could once again give fealty to a transcendent ideal, the depression would be conquered as once the armies of the Kaiser had been. Charles Beard proposed a "heroic national effort" that would leave people "richer in goods—and still more important, in patriotic spirit." Many conceived the New Deal not simply as a new kind of economic mobilization but also, as the war had been, a venture in "nation-saving." One of the New Deal experiments was later to be lauded because it had led to "a new baptism of patriotism and an increased consciousness of national unity."

• • •

There was scarcely a New Deal act or agency that did not owe something to the experience of World War I. The Tennessee Valley Authority —the most ambitious New Deal experiment in regional planning—grew out of the creation of a government-operated nitrate and electric-power project at Muscle Shoals during and after the war. In his message asking for creation of the TVA, President Roosevelt concluded: "In short, this power development of war days leads logically to national planning."[2]

• • •

The public-housing movement of the thirties had first come of age during the war. In World War I, Congress authorized the Emergency Fleet Corporation and the United States Housing Corporation to provide housing for war workers. The war established the principle of federal intervention in housing, and it trained architects like Robert Kohn, who served as chief of production of the housing division of the U.S. Shipping Board. After the armistice, Kohn observed: ". . . The war has put housing 'on the map' in this country." In 1933, President Roosevelt named Kohn to head the New Deal's first public-housing venture. Imaginative wartime experiments with garden-city ideas paved the way for the greenbelt towns of the thirties, while the rural resettlement and subsistence homestead projects of the New Deal reaped the harvest of seeds planted by Elwood Mead and Franklin K. Lane in the war years.

• • •

The New Deal's program of farm price supports owed something to the wartime Food Administration and even more to a decade of proselytization by George Peek, a hard-bitten farm-belt agitator who had served as "a sort of generalissimo of industry" under the War Industries Board. Peek's war experience with the ways government could benefit industry had led him to argue that the government should give the same measure of aid to the distressed farmer. Frustrated in the twenties by Republican Presidents in his campaign to win support for McNary-Haugenism, Peek pinned his hopes on the election of Franklin Roosevelt in 1932. . . . Roosevelt's victory touched off a serious debate over how to curb farm surpluses which, after months of wrangling, ended in the passage of the Agricultural Adjustment Act in the spring of 1933. To head the new Agricultural Adjustment Administration, Roosevelt named George Peek. "To him, with his war experience, this whole thing clicks into shape," Peek's wife noted, "and some of the fine men of the country are coming to his call as they did in 1917, and with the same high purpose."

• • •

[2] The special form of the TVA—the government corporation endowed with many of the powers and much of the flexibility of a business corporation—had first found wide acceptance in the war.

While the CCC,[3] the AAA, the TVA, housing, economy, and banking legislation all shared in the war legacy, it was the National Recovery Administration that was the keystone of the early New Deal, and the NRA rested squarely on the War Industries Board example. The National Industrial Recovery bill, modeled on WIB procedures, wove together a series of schemes for government-business co-ordination of the kind that had prevailed in the war. . . . When the President commissioned Raymond Moley to frame legislation for industrial recovery, Moley asked General Hugh Johnson, who in World War I had functioned as a liaison between the Army and the War Industries Board, to take over for him. "Nobody can do it better than you," Moley coaxed. "You're familiar with the only comparable thing that's ever been done—the work of the War Industries Board." The recovery bill, drafted by Johnson and others, won Senate approval by only the narrowest of margins; conservatives foresaw that the measure would enhance the power of the state and Progressives believed the proposal would encourage cartelization. Franklin Roosevelt was more sanguine. When the President signed the recovery act of June 16, he commented: "Many good men voted this new charter with misgivings. I do not share these doubts. I had part in the great cooperation of 1917 and 1918 and it is my faith that we can count on our industry once more to join in our general purpose to lift this new threat. . . ."

Before labor would agree to the industrial-recovery program, it insisted on the same degree of government recognition of the right to organize as it had enjoyed in World War I. In December, 1932, shortly after he learned that Frances Perkins would be the new Secretary of Labor, Sidney Hillman sent her a memorandum which urged the government to pursue the kinds of policies the War Labor Board had initiated. In framing the recovery bill, W. Jett Lauck, who had been secretary of the War Labor Board, served as spokesman for John L. Lewis's United Mine Workers. Lauck, who sponsored a plan for "a national board composed of labor modeled after the War Labor Board," played a prominent part in shaping the labor provisions of the legislation. When the national industrial-recovery bill emerged from the drafting room, it incorporated the pivotal section 7(a) which granted labor's demand for recognition of the right of collective bargaining. The essential provisions of 7(a), noted Edwin Witte, were "but restatements" of principles first recognized by the National War Labor Board.

Franklin Roosevelt had not only had a prominent part in framing

---

[3] The preceding omitted portion discussed the Civilian Conservation Corps. [*Editor's note.*]

World War I labor policies, but had, as Gerald Nash has pointed out, "sketched out the blueprint for the War Labor Policies Board which was modeled on his directive." To staff the National Labor Board of 1933, the President named men he had first encountered in developing war labor programs. William Leiserson, executive secretary of the board, had been Roosevelt's personal adviser on labor affairs in 1918. In formulating labor policy—from interpreting 7(a) through the adoption and administration of the Wagner Act—Roosevelt and his lieutenants drew heavily on war precedents. The war agencies had established the basic principles of the New Deal labor program: that workers had the right to unionize, that they must not be discharged for union activity, and that Presidential boards could restrain employers from denying such rights. More than this, they had evolved the procedure of plant elections to determine bargaining representatives which was to be the crucial instrumentality employed by Roosevelt's labor boards.

· · ·

To man the New Deal agencies, Roosevelt turned to the veterans of the war mobilization. Top NRA officials included Johnson's chief of staff, John Hancock, who had managed the War Industries Board's naval industrial program; Charles F. Horner, the genius of the Liberty Loan drive; Leo Wolman, who had headed the section on production statistics of the War Industries Board; and Major General Clarence Charles Williams, who had been Chief of Ordnance in charge of the vast war purchasing. Many other New Dealers had had their first taste of government service during the war. The first Administrator for Public Works, Colonel Donald H. Sawyer, had built cantonments; Felix Frankfurter had chaired the War Labor Policies Board; Captain Leon Henderson of Ordnance had served with the War Industries Board; and Senator Joseph Guffey had worked in the War Industries Board on the conservation of oil. For many, the summer of 1933 seemed like old times. "Washington is a hectic place," wrote Isador Lubin in August. "The hotels are filled, and the restaurants remind me very much of war times. One cannot go into the Cosmos Club without meeting half a dozen persons whom he knew during the war."

· · ·

The processes of New Deal government owed much to the war legacy. The war provided a precedent for the concentration of executive authority, for the responsibility of government for the state of the economy, and

for the role of Washington as the arbiter among social groups. It origi-
nated the practice of shunting aside the regular line agencies and creating
new organizations with dramatic alphabetical titles. When the RFC, the
first of the new agencies, was established, one periodical reported:
"R.F.C., of course, is Reconstruction Finance Corporation, and the newspapers have fallen into the war-time habit of using the simple initials
instead of the rather cumbersome full name of this anti-hard-times organization." The war offered a precedent, too, for setting up co-ordinating
bodies like the National Emergency Council headed by Frank Walker.
Not least in importance, the war experience was used to justify the New
Deal's emergency legislation in the courts.

* * *

The New Dealers resorted to the analogue of war, because in America
the sense of community is weak, the distrust of the state strong. Up to a
point, the metaphor of war and the precedent of World War I proved
invaluable. They helped provide a feeling of national solidarity which
made possible the New Deal's greatest achievement: its success in "nation-
saving," in mending the social fabric. The heritage of World War I
justified the New Deal's claim to represent an overarching national interest to which business and other parochial interests must conform. The
war proved that, at a time of crisis, the power of private individuals with
money to turn the nation's resources to their own benefit could be
limited by the prior claim of providing a "social minimum." Since the
war mobilization had brought to fruition much of progressivism, it offered
a useful example for the New Dealers, and since the wartime control of
industry went much further than earlier efforts in recognizing the place
of the twentieth-century state, it was especially pertinent for some of the
problems the New Deal confronted.

Yet in other respects the war analogue proved either treacherous or
inadequate. The very need to employ imagery which was so often inappro-
priate revealed both an impoverished tradition of reform and the reluctance of the nation to come to terms with the leviathan state. Only in war
or in a crisis likened to war was it possible to put aside inhibiting doctrines, create a sense of national homogeneity, and permit the government to act in the national interest. But once the war ended, or the sense
of crisis dissipated, traditional doctrines once again prevailed. The
country had yet to find a way to organize collective action save in war
or its surrogate. Nor had it faced up to the real problems of the relation
of order to liberty which the power of the twentieth-century state
creates. . . .

The Reign of Terror in the Middle West

ROBERT L. MORLAN

The pressure of war did not simply advance governmental control of the economy and stimulate renewed Progressive efforts. For reasons suggested in the introduction, the War also engendered a spirit of intolerance directed at radicals, dissenters, and minority groups. In the following chapter from a history of the Nonpartisan League, a midwestern farmers' movement begun in 1915, Robert L. Morlan describes one facet of this intolerance. He presents the most revealing evidence in print of the way that conservatives were able to use chauvinism, anti-German hysteria, and even terroristic methods to attack and descredit radical and Progressive organizations. The federal government itself mounted sustained legal attacks against Socialist leaders and the radical Industrial Workers of the World, because of their overt opposition to the War. However, Mr. Morlan discloses that the main thrust against alleged radicalism in the Middle West came, not from the Washington Administration, but from conservatives with very particular goals in view.

From Robert L. Morlan, *Political Prairie Fire: The Nonpartisan League, 1915–1922*, Minneapolis: University of Minnesota Press, 1955, pp. 152–159, 162–173, 179–182. Copyright © 1955 by the University of Minnesota. The footnotes in the original text have been omitted.

IN THE EARLY DAYS OF LEAGUE ORGANIZING IN MINNESOTA ITS
activities received relatively little attention, and in a number of
instances there was interested cooperation by village and city commercial clubs in providing facilities for farmers' meetings. As the strength
of the organization grew, however, so also did that of the opposition.
The attack was led by the Twin Cities newspapers, whose views were
frequently copied by many country weeklies, and the attitude of the
Public Safety Commission was also extremely influential. Business interests
throughout the state were given to understand that the Nonpartisan
League was fundamentally disloyal and that any meetings it might sponsor
could automatically be assumed to be seditious.

In vain did the League endeavor to concentrate on domestic issues,
insisting that there was no dispute as to the need for effective and speedy
prosecution of the war. Those issues the opposition resolutely ignored,
other than by taking an occasional slap at "socialism," and the anti-League
press hammered one theme to the exclusion of all else—this was a time
for unity, and agitators who stirred up discontent or in any way challenged the status quo could be nothing else than traitorous. The loyalty
issue was a handy and potent weapon against a political opponent who
had the popular side of an argument, and the length to which this opposition and a fanatical brand of "patriotism" were carried constitutes a
sordid chapter in the history of Minnesota.

The League had planned and announced a series of fall meetings at
towns scattered over southern and central Minnesota, designed to secure
new members and to serve as "pep rallies" for those already members.
At the same time there were carefully made "loyalty meetings"—collec-
tions for the Red Cross were invariably taken, high production was urged,
and the purchase of Liberty Bonds was advocated, though it was always
emphasized how much more just conscription of wealth would be. By
the time this series of mass meetings got under way, the lines were fairly
clearly drawn and most townspeople had been conditioned against the
League. A brief account of a few of these meetings gives some idea of
the sharpness of the conflict, even in the initial stages, the kind of conditions under which it was necessary for the League to operate, and the
major role played by misunderstanding and false publicity.

Trouble began with the first meeting, which had been scheduled for
October 4 in Lake City (Wabasha County). The commercial club and
various businessmen had put pressure on the mayor to prohibit the
meeting, and the owner of the hall that had been rented was forced to
refuse to open it. Some two hundred fifty farmers were soon milling in

the street, and violence threatened when someone caused a fire hose to be laid out conspicuously along the sidewalk as an obvious threat. Townley,[1] however, advised them not to insist on their right of assembly and announced that the meeting would be held that night at Dumfries, about twenty miles distant. Most of the farmers had to go home for evening chores, but by eight o'clock the Dumfries hall was packed, not with two hundred fifty, but with more than four hundred attentive listeners. Among those present were the sheriff and the county attorney of Wabasha County, both of whom stated publicly at the conclusion that it had clearly been a "patriotic" meeting and that the farmers were entitled to assemble freely wherever they wished. The president of the Farmers and Traders Bank of Wabasha then took it upon himself to invite the speakers to hold a meeting in that city on their first open date. Four days later Townley and former Congressman Charles A. Lindbergh addressed a crowded city auditorium there without incident.

The commercial club of Litchfield had held a special session in advance of the League meeting scheduled for that village on October 9, and had petitioned Governor Burnquist to prevent the meeting. The Public Safety Commission, however, had had a stenographer at all League gatherings and was well aware that there were no grounds for such action. Despite the fact that a local paper reported the commercial club move in such a manner as to give the impression that the meeting would be prohibited, farmers flocked in to fill the opera house and listen to three hours of speeches. The sheriffs of Meeker and Kandiyohi counties were present and both agreed that nothing objectionable had been said. The Kandiyohi sheriff had come because a meeting was scheduled for Willmar on a later date, and he wished to determine his proper course of action. He asked Townley at the end of the meeting if he would make the same kind of speech in Willmar.

"Brother, I'll make just the same kind of speech that I made today, and that speech that I made today is just the kind of a speech that I've been making for the last six months," replied Townley.

"Well, that's all right," said the sheriff. "What you said there today is just what we believe in."

A meeting had been scheduled for the next day in Mankato, but two days before the date the owner of the hall returned the money to the farmers who had rented it, saying that businessmen and local politicians had threatened him with loss of business if he permitted the League to use the hall. The owner of the local opera house was approached and

---

[1] Arthur C. ' Townley, founder and president of the Nonpartisan League. [*Editor's note.*]

agreed to rent if the city authorities would approve. This they refused to do, Mayor Champlin reportedly commenting that the League was led by "a bunch of I.W.W.'s." The Mankato papers announced that the meeting would not be held and told the farmers that there was no point in coming to town. Nevertheless, early afternoon found more than five hundred farmers thronging the streets, especially in front of the city hall. Police officers tried to hustle them along, but met with strong resentment. Threats of no more trading in Mankato and "wait till the next election" were heard on all sides, but one farmer who had driven forty miles to attend perhaps best summed up the feelings of all when told that the meeting was not to be permitted. "Ain't farmers legal?" he asked.

Meanwhile arrangements were being made to hold the meeting that night in Nicollet, some fifteen miles away. But word came that county authorities would not allow the meeting, so the farmers in charge stopped at St. Peter, the county seat, where the sheriff informed them that the safety commission had refused permission. It turned out that he referred to the county safety commission, headed by Herman Olson, a St. Peter banker. Olson admitted that he knew nothing personally of the League but that he had read in the Twin Cities papers that it was seditious. Farmers who knew him assured him that this was false and invited both Olson and the sheriff to attend. To this he finally agreed, and the meeting was approved.

There had been little opportunity for notice of the change of location, but the "grapevine" had been functioning and instead of the five hundred farmers who had come to Mankato more than a thousand swarmed into Nicollet. No hall in town could begin to accommodate a crowd of this size, and the meeting was consequently held outdoors. It was cold and the wind came in chilling blasts which cut through the warmest clothing, yet the grim-faced farmers stood in the open air for nearly three hours while Arthur Townley talked of the need to battle autocracy at home as well as abroad. Suddenly he brought forth his flair for the dramatic. He spoke emotionally of the tremendous difficulties the farmers were facing in building their organization, of how they were being driven from towns like cattle and falsely branded traitors to their country. The interests fighting the League were prepared to spend millions to beat it, he said, and they would feel that they had gotten off cheaply if they had a chance to buy off the members.

"We could get the money," cried Townley. "What if I could get you $1600 for each $16 membership—would you sell?"

"No! No! No!" shouted back the crowd. Then someone yelled "We'll stick!" and a thousand voices roared the old North Dakota battle cry into the icy wind.

Herman Olson was convinced. He thanked Townley and promised to tell the attorney general and the Public Safety Commission that it had been a loyal meeting. Furthermore, when the sheriff of Nobles County the next day threatened to prevent a meeting at Worthington, Olson on his own initiative called him by telephone to assure him that the League was "all right."

Meanwhile, a meeting of county sheriffs was held in St. Paul, to which the governor sent a representative to answer questions on how to handle the League problem. They were told that "if a riot seemed imminent, the responsibility for the outcome of any meeting rested upon the sheriff, and that it would be for the sheriff to take action to prevent such riots." Although there had been no instance in that state or any other of the farmers rioting, all mob action having come from the opposition, riots immediately became imminent in a number of counties whenever League meetings were to be held. In areas where the League was strongly organized, primarily the western part of the state, they were rarely molested.

On October 5, Townley received an interesting letter signed by Louis Keane, secretary of the Otter Tail County Public Safety Association, which read:

Information has reached this office to the effect that you contemplate speaking here in this county on Octo. 20.

I am instructed to notify you that this Association will not tolerate any kind of talk here except that which honors our flag and the country for which it stands.

So you will construe this notice as an invitation *not to come*.

If after the receipt of this notice you persist in trying to talk here we have made arrangements with our Mayor who has given orders to the police force not to interfere if small boys (and others) use ancient eggs and other missiles where with to punctuate your discourse.

This open threat of mob violence made by officials pledged to preserve law and order Townley was eager to challenge. The mayor of Fergus Falls, where the meeting was to be held, decided, however, to forestall any incidents of this sort and forbade the holding of any meeting at which Townley was to speak. Since it was the policy of the League never to defy public authorities, arrangements were made for former Congressmen Lindbergh and Manahan to speak and they were not interfered with. The Fergus Falls opera house was filled to capacity, and there was but one dissenting vote on a resolution calling upon Governor Burnquist to remove the mayor for his illegal action.

The following day, Sunday, October 21, when the farmers came to the city of Detroit they found the hall where the meeting was to be held locked and were informed that here too the mayor had forbidden Townley to speak within the city limits. Furious, they accepted the invitation of a Dr. Cowles to use his lawn, just outside the city, and for two hours hundreds of what one farmer termed "these free American citizens that the gates of Detroit were shut against" stood in a snow-storm to listen to the president of their League. Surely this was more than common attentiveness to political oratory.

As a matter of fact, it seems likely that such tactics as these tended to gain converts for the League, which stoutly maintained from beginning to end that there was really no loyalty issue involved and that this was simply barefaced political persecution by officeholders who feared for their jobs in 1918. Certainly nothing was achieved by preventing meetings except the fostering of further ill-will and a deepening of the town versus country antagonism. The meetings were always held elsewhere, and who, after all, was being protected? If speakers actually did violate the laws they would then properly have been subject to arrest, but there were certainly no grounds for this censorship in advance by overly officious local authorities. There were many instances in which farmers refused to return to towns where their meetings had been banned, and merchants were forced to apologize and promise a changed policy in order to regain their lost trade. The entire situation was but a part of the almost insane hysteria of the times.

As fall progressed and winter came on, the breaking up of League meetings either by local officials or by mobs was almost standard practice, and violence became more and more common. League organizers and speakers in some counties were beaten, tarred and feathered, and threatened with lynching, which in several instances almost occurred. League members were subjected to personal assaults and destruction of property, and one farmer with a German name was "deported" from Rock County —taken across a state line clothed in hot tar and told never to return.

Merchants with League sympathies found their store fronts painted yellow and their windows smashed. Professors at the University of Minnesota suspected of pro-League attitudes found that their desks had been rifled at night, and it was later discovered that dictographs had been placed in certain classrooms. The editor of the *Park Region Echo*, who had reported favorably on a League meeting, came to his office in the morning to find the door open, his linotype smashed, his press damaged beyond repair, and his correspondence files stolen. Many a gathering of farmers was greeted with mud, rotten eggs, stones, buckets of yellow paint, or the blast of a fire hose, which in one case was said to have torn a six-month-old baby from its mother's arms. In more than one case Home Guards were utilized in breaking up these meetings. Local law enforcement officials in a number of instances openly threatened the use of force against League organizing or speaking, yet did nothing to restrain the lawless actions of self-styled "loyalists."

This state of affairs, which George Creel later termed a "policy of brutal intolerance," seemingly had the tacit approval of the state officials, and the Public Safety Commission at one time went so far as to advocate mobbings. A publicity release of January 19, sent to editors of the state on official stationery, was headed "One Cure for Disloyalty—A Cure That Is Used in Many Cases with Good Effect." It told the unlikely story of a man in a small Minnesota town who allegedly tore a Red Cross button off another man's coat and threw it in a spittoon. In a moment he was set upon and "beaten to a pulp by a crowd of loyalists." When he recovered he was promptly fined $100 and jailed. The Public Safety Commission referred to the incident as follows:

> This had a very salutary effect on the balance of the disloyal element and they began to seek information on the war and its causes in a conscientious manner. The time is coming when even a disloyal utterance or lukewarm attitude will be resented by the American people in every section. There is no "halfway" citizenship that can live in these times.

There was a significant correlation county by county between the attitudes of local newspapers and the existence or nonexistence of mob violence. In places where such action occurred the papers were almost invariably in the habit of either actively encouraging it or excusing it as "natural" in wartime. The *Rush City Post,* for example, editorialized in March:

> There is something refreshing in the [manner] in which direct punishment is being inflicted upon numerous disloyalists at street gatherings and public meetings throughout the country. Mob law is mighty effective when properly administered and usually carries justice in its right hand.

In a slightly more moderate vein the *Hinckley Enterprise* commented: "As much as we deprecate the violence of the acts that prevented a disloyal meeting, we had much rather be apologizing for the violence of loyalists than for the disloyal actions which cause them . . ."

The standard argument of those seeking to prevent or break up League meetings was to the effect that this was "not the time to organize." The American people, they said, should now be concerned solely with the winning of the war; politics or economic problems should not be permitted to divert their attention. In response to the League's complaint that everyone else was already organized, they agreed that of course the farmers had a right to organize but "not at a time like this." Oddly enough there seemed to be no similar feeling in regard to the various organizations which were springing up in opposition to the League, nor could it be said that in North Dakota, where the shoe was on the other foot by virtue of a League-dominated state administration, there was any noticeable cessation of political activity designed to unseat incumbents.

By March of 1918 nineteen Minnesota counties had completely barred all meetings of the League, thus by local fiat suspending the right of free assemblage and in effect denying the right of political action to a large segment of the population. Up to that time no fewer than forty scheduled meetings had been prevented by local officials, and no one kept track of the number interfered with by self-appointed guardians of the public welfare.

• • •

Throughout the winter months Governor Burnquist was besieged by a steady stream of resolutions from farmers' groups all over the state pleading for enforcement of the laws, demanding protection of peaceful assembly, and asking the removal of local officials who had prevented meetings or permitted mob violence. On February 19 a delegation of League members, headed by Magnus Johnson of Kimball and A. C. Welch of Glencoe, both members of the Minnesota legislature, appeared at the governor's office and read a letter which set forth a long series of "outrages" and demanded action by the state's chief executive. It minced no words:

The rights of citizens to meet in peaceful assemblage, to discuss matters of public concern, to be immune from unlawful assaults, and to be secure in their liberties, have been flagrantly, repeatedly and notoriously violated . . .

Law abiding citizens . . . have been watched and followed from town to town by persons assuming authority to prevent such lawful pursuits; have been publicly and falsely vilified and accused of crime, and have been openly threatened with violence, torture, and death.

Public officials have joined in this carnival of intimidation and oppression . . .

Men have been coerced, assaulted, kidnapped; law has been denied; passion has supplanted reason; riot has been invited; the process of social order has been menaced by the approach of anarchy.

These things, Sir, have not happened in a corner nor in the dark. They are notorious. A period of nearly six months has not sufficed to exhaust the malignity of these assaults upon the peace and dignity of the State, and the scenes of their occurrence are widely scattered throughout its territory.

The circumstances point to the existence of a lawless propaganda instigated and sustained by persons higher up, working through the agency of the immediate actors. . . . But whether or not there be a conspiracy against the public peace and order, it is clear and undenied that these things have occurred, and their continuing occurrence demands instant corrective action at your hands.

On March 2 the attorney general ruled that the charges made by the delegation against the sheriff and county attorney of Jackson County, the sheriff of Rice County, and the acting sheriff of Ramsey County were insufficient to warrant their removal, and Governor Burnquist dismissed the whole matter as the work of "troublemakers."

Judge McGee, the chairman of the Public Safety Commission, was reported as having later said to Magnus Johnson: "I came into the Governor's office when you were reading that, and if I had known what you were reading and had had a club, I would have knocked your brains out."

On February 26 the state executive committee of the Minnesota League prepared a resolution concerning the "intolerable" conditions in the state which asked the aid and advice of the national officers. Townley forwarded this to Governor Burnquist, asking three questions:

FIRST: Are local officers in the municipalities of the State to be permitted to prevent meetings of the League?

SECOND: Are members of the League to be denied the protection of the laws?

THIRD: Is the National Nonpartisan League to be regarded by the executive and peace officers of the State as an outlaw?

Burnquist cautiously replied that no official had a right to prevent the holding of any legal and loyal meeting, that every citizen was entitled to the protection of the laws, and that insofar as the League complied with the laws of the state and nation it was not an outlaw. Incensed by what he termed these generalities and legal truisms, Townley restated the questions in more detail and requested a reply "specifically without any innuendo, implication, evasion, or equivocation," and a statement of the manner of noncompliance with the laws. There was no reply.

Having apparently failed in their appeals to the state officials, the League next turned to the United States district attorney, and then in April the national and state executive committees published their *Memorial to the Congress of the United States Concerning Conditions in Minnesota, 1918.* This volume, and one to the President of the United States which was identical except for the introduction, claimed with extensive supporting evidence that citizens of the United States were being deprived of their constitutional rights and asked the protection of national officials since state officials refused to act. The national administration, however, had neither the time, the personnel, nor the inclination to attempt to intervene in this highly charged situation, which it considered to be primarily a local political battle.

In late March the National Committee on Public Information agreed at Townley's request to furnish "loyalty speakers" to deliver a series of patriotic addresses under League sponsorship, particularly in areas in which it was believed that support of the war might be lukewarm. Local officials in Cottonwood, Jackson, Martin, and Watonwan counties refused to permit such meetings as long as they were sponsored by the League, and in this they were backed up by the state administration. In vain did Chairman Creel argue with the Public Safety Commission that if they were right as to the existence of disloyal elements it was to those localities that these speakers should go; there was nothing to be gained by preaching to those already converted. Permission was still refused. Creel later summed up the situation in a letter to Charles Edward Russell:

. . . It was at Mr. Townley's request that I prepared to send speakers into the Northwest—men and women able to talk of the war as they had seen it, or else able to discuss America's aims from every point of view.

It was what we were doing in every state in the Union in our effort to remove misunderstanding, to promote unity, and to kindle enthusiasm.

It was such speakers that the state administration of Minnesota barred absolutely. It was not that they questioned the loyalty of the speakers; in fact, they asked for the use of them in their own campaigns. It was simply the case that they did not mean to let the Nonpartisan League hold meetings of any kind, even loyalty meetings. What stood clear in my mind then, as it stands clear today, is that Democrats and Republicans alike feared the political power of the Nonpartisan League and did not want it to be given any reputation for loyalty. In plain words, they preferred that the Nonpartisan League should be disloyal rather than loyal, in order that they might be provided with a campaign weapon.

In mid-March the Leader uncovered a letter written by Governor Burnquist to a man in Nebraska in which he categorically stated that the League was "hindering the prosecution of the war." The Leader promptly boiled over. This, it said, was either a deliberate untruth or else the governor should be removed from office for failing to do his duty—there was ample power in the Public Safety Commission to abolish the League: "Why do you let an organization that is hindering the war continue, governor?"

The League persistently contended that it was fully as essential to fight for democracy at home as in Germany; that it was completely inconsistent for the Public Safety Commission to spend huge sums of money to tell the people that this was a war for democracy and liberty while at the same time it ignored or actively encouraged the suppression of democracy in Minnesota. The commission's words would ring more true, it said, if accompanied by action against "autocracy and kaiserism in some of the small towns of Minnesota."

A bill by Senator Chamberlain of Oregon that provided for placing all cases involving the espionage act under the jurisdiction of military authorities came up for hearings in April, and Judge McGee, chairman of the Public Safety Commission and federal fuel administrator for Minnesota, went to Washington to testify. His remarks before the committee were startling almost beyond belief:

> The United States Department of Justice in Minnesota has been a ghastly failure. The United States District Attorney in Minnesota is patriotic but he lacks a fighting stomach . . .
>
> A Non-Partisan League lecturer is a traitor every time. In other words, no matter what he says or does, a League worker is a traitor . . .
>
> Where we made a mistake was in not establishing a firing squad in the first days of the war. We should now get busy and have that firing squad working overtime. Wait until the long causalty lists begin to come in and the Minnesota woods will not be dense enough to hide the traitors who will meet punishment for their crimes. These men who are fighting our soldiers and stabbing them in the back are going to die.
>
> The nation's life is at stake. The government has no more conception of the state of affairs in Minnesota than a child unborn. In these days the judges should not think in terms of peace. What we need is a military court. You can't fool the military court, but you can't depend on juries . . .
>
> The disloyal element in Minnesota is largely among the German-Swedish people. The nation blundered at the start of the war in not dealing severely with these vipers.

There was immediately a wave of protest in Minnesota at McGee's indictment of the Germans and Swedes and his statement that Minnesota was a hotbed of disloyalty. Newspapers which had at first played up his testimony found it necessary to say that his views were "in sharp contrast" to those of Governor Burnquist, who believed that "Minnesota is as loyal as any state in the union, people of Swedish extraction particularly." On April 20 President Wilson sent a strongly worded message to the chairman of the Senate Judiciary Committee, which was influential in killing the "court martial bill":

> I am wholly and unalterably opposed to such legislation . . . I think it not only unconstitutional, but that in character it would put us nearly on the level of the very people we are fighting and affecting to despise. It would be altogether inconsistent with the spirit and practice of America, and . . . I think it is unnecessary and uncalled for.

"Again," said the *Leader,* "the confidence of the American people in President Wilson has been proved well placed."

The differences in attitude toward the Nonpartisan League on the part of the national government and the state of Minnesota were striking. The former at all times cooperated with the League, considering it an important spokesman for the northwest farmer, while the latter looked upon it as virtually an outlaw organization. Department of Justice agents frequented League meetings in all parts of the state, yet never made an arrest, while in some counties local officials were locking up their speakers on sight. Attempts to get the United States to prosecute League leaders repeatedly failed. League publications were granted second-class mailing privileges at a time when regulations provided that publications in this class must contain nothing in policy or in purpose which in any way might hinder the war effort. They were also allowed the one-cent rate to American forces in France, but at the same time arrests were being made in Minnesota on the grounds that League literature was seditious. It is scarcely open to question that the fact that 1918 was a state election year was a highly significant factor in this situation.

George Creel summarized accurately the attitude of the national government in a letter of May 13, 1918, to John A. Simpson, president of the Oklahoma Farmers' Union, who had written the National Committee on Public Information asking if there were any reason why a loyal farmer should not join the League:

It is not true that the federal government is pressing the Nonpartisan League in any manner, or that the federal government considers it an act of disloyalty to be a member of this League.

The federal government is not concerned with the political, economic, or industrial beliefs of any organization at a time like this, insisting only that every individual stand behind this war, believing absolutely in the justice of America's position.

The Nonpartisan League, by resolution and by organized effort, has given this pledge of loyalty. North Dakota, controlled by this organization politically, has as fine a record of war support as any other commonwealth in the Union. Mr. Baer, its representative in the lower house, has never even been criticized for a single utterance that might be termed disloyal.

Mr. Townley is under indictment in Minnesota, and there is a very bitter fight being made on the League in that state by certain groups. With this, the government has nothing to do, refusing absolutely to take part in these local differences.

Sedition and discouraging enlistments were of course crimes under United States statutes, but Minnesota had passed similar laws supplementing those of the United States, and while the government against which the alleged crimes were perpetrated took no action, the state in a number of instances made arrests under its statute, especially in the months preceding the primaries.

In one of the first of these cases to come to trial, L. W. Martin, a League organizer, was indicted in Red Wing seven months after the speech on which the indictment was based. After three days of testimony and argument, Martin was acquitted on the first ballot, but the newspapers which had given the matter wide publicity, implying that his guilt was obvious, for the most part gave inconsequential notice to the acquittal. The prosecutor had made the mistake of asking Martin to repeat what he had said, and he thereupon launched into a full-fledged speech to the crowded courtroom. It was reported that after the acquittal a half-dozen farmers from the audience came up to Martin to ask for membership blanks.

On February 28, 1918, County Attorney Albert R. Allen of Martin County, one of the counties which had consistently barred all League meetings, issued complaints against A. C. Townley and Joseph Gilbert, charging that they had discouraged enlistments in Minnesota by circulating a pamphlet entitled *The Nonpartisan League; Its Origin, Purposes, and Methods of Organization*. This was the pamphlet which contained the League war resolutions and Congressman Baer's public statement at the time of his election, although the great majority of its space was devoted to the League's economic and political program. It had been in circulation since the preceding June with no complaint from the national government, which had, in fact, granted mailing privileges for it. Moreover, much of its "war program" had by now become official United States policy. A later indictment also included the resolutions of the Producers and Consumers Convention.

County Attorney Allen was one of the state's most vehement "superpatriots," a young man with a reputation as a fiery orator and as an almost fanatical opponent of the Nonpartisan League and all it stood for. The depths of this antagonism are indicated by the fact that in the fall of 1917 he had gone so far as to demand of the state bar association that it investigate the possible necessity of disbarring and perhaps impeaching Governor Burnquist on the grounds that he was failing to suppress "rampant disloyalty and sedition" in the state. Subsequently, in a speech before a county attorneys' convention in Minneapolis, he delivered himself of a tirade which was clearly the reasoned view of a dispassionate and unprejudiced law enforcement official:

God forbid that the prosecuting attorneys of America should slumber in the presence of this disloyalty. The League is the Kaiser's hope. Let us resolve that this criminal, disloyal political club that brazenly seeks to mislead thoughtless innocents, associate them with traitors and spies, corrupt our officials, capture our country and lead her blindfolded by the route of Russian bolshevikism to a condition of Prussianized slavery, shall not go slyly or successfully about its nefarious work.

After issuing the complaints, Allen instructed Sheriff W. S. Carver to go to St. Paul, arrest Townley and Gilbert, and bring them back to Fairmont, the county seat of Martin County, to await trial. Carver proceeded to place them under arrest, whereupon they at once demanded to be taken before the district court of Ramsey County to apply for bail. Carver insisted that he had been ordered to take them to Fairmont, but after receiving legal advice as to the rights of his prisoners he took them to the court where bonds of $3000 each were furnished and they were released.

Returning to Fairmont empty-handed, the hapless sheriff met a thoroughly disgusted Allen, who insisted that the Ramsey County court had no jurisdiction and ordered Carver and Deputy Sheriff Roepke to go back to St. Paul and secure the prisoners. Townley in the meantime had left town on a speaking engagement but Gilbert was available and was again taken into custody. Carver decided to wait for a time in the hope that Townley might return, but in order to prevent Gilbert from taking any legal action to free himself again, he sent Roepke and Gilbert by automobile to Mendota, where after two or three hours' wait they caught the train to Fairmont. In the interim, League attorneys had heard of the events and had secured from the district court of Ramsey County a writ of habeas corpus, which was promptly served upon Sheriff Carver, ordering him to produce Gilbert in St. Paul at once. Frightened by this time, Carver wired Roepke to return Gilbert to St. Paul, but the deputy, who received the telegram at Lake Crystal, suspected that it was a fake and continued to Fairmont.

Gilbert spent the night in jail, having refused to let Allen go his bail, and in the morning, to his great amusement, the sour-faced county attorney placed him on the train back to St. Paul. The following day, Sheriff Carver having at last produced Gilbert before the Ramsey County court, the court ordered him released on his original bond and he was directed to appear at Fairmont for trial the following Monday. Gilbert immediately filed suit against the Martin County officials on charges of kidnapping and false imprisonment, which was later settled out of court with a payment of $275.

When the case came to trial, the attorneys for Townley and Gilbert at once entered demurrers to the charges, contending that they did not constitute a cause of action, that the resolutions and statements involved were so plainly patriotic that they could not be used as a basis for such charges, and that the resolutions and statements were almost in the same language used by President Wilson in his recent speeches and messages to Congress. Judge Tifft overruled the demurrers, but agreed, over the passionate protest of the county attorney, to certify two questions directly to the state Supreme Court:

(1) Is the section on which the indictments are based within the subject expressed in the title of the act?
(2) Do the facts constitute a violation of that section?

While the case was pending before the Supreme Court, the indictments were used for all they were worth by the anti-League forces. News that Townley and Gilbert had been indicted for antiwar activity, with guilt customarily assumed, was given the widest publicity throughout the entire country, but especially in those states which the League was attempting to organize. The standard "proof" given of the disloyal nature of the League was that its leaders were under indictment for "sedition." The League's claim that this publicity cost it tens of thousands of votes in the 1918 primaries does not seem unduly farfetched.

The case had been certified to the Supreme Court in March, but it was not until July 5, several days after the Minnesota primary election, that the court handed down its decision, written by Judge Quinn, whose home, appropriately enough, was in Fairmont. The court answered the first question in the affirmative without detailed discussion, and then, in consideration of the second, proceeded to sustain the demurrers filed by the League attorneys. Great emphasis had been placed by the prosecution upon one paragraph in particular from the resolutions of the Producers and Consumers Convention which read:

The moving cause of this world war was and is political autocracy used to perpetuate and extend industrial autocracy. It is the struggle of political overlords to extend and perpetuate their power to rob and exploit their fellowmen. Autocratic rulers who have robbed and exploited the fathers and mothers now slaughter the children for the single purpose of further intrenching themselves in their infamous position and securing and legalizing their possession of the fruits of others' toil and thrusting the world under the yoke of political autocracy, which is ever the shield and the mask of industrial autocracy.

The court decided to "play it straight," and accepted the contentions of the League attorneys that obviously this applied to the German-Austrian autocracy, since we had no autocracy in this country:

. . . the language, properly considered and taken in the light of the surrounding pertinent facts, cannot be held as tending to discourage enlistment in the army or otherwise to advocate that assistance should not be rendered the government in the prosecution of the war . . .

John Quinn remarked that since it is the federal government whose authority is challenged by seditious action, the rules as to what constitutes such action should properly be determined in the United States courts, and noted that "it is perhaps not out of place to, say that the resolutions have not yet attracted the attention of the federal authorities." Regarding the League's war resolutions themselves, the court concluded:

The resolutions taken as a whole appear to be nothing more serious than a rhetorical, and somewhat flamboyant, platform upon which a certain class of citizens are solicited to join an organization whose avowed purpose is the amelioration of the alleged evils of present economic conditions, and to bring about a more equal distribution of the wealth of the world among all classes of mankind. The pursuit of this object does not violate the statute in question . . .

The court cannot inject by inference matter of substance between the lines of the resolutions, and predicate a conviction thereon, for the fact and not the prosecutor's inferences must be the basis of a conviction under the statute.

The *Leader* hailed the decision as a sweeping and complete vindication of the League, which should put at rest for all time the false charges of disloyalty. It was overly sanguine. The day after the decision the *St. Paul Pioneer Press* gave front-page prominence to a statement of County Attorney Allen's to the effect that despite the decision the case had been a success, since it had convinced the people of the disloyalty of the League and had completely discredited both Townley and the organization. Perhaps Albert Allen had achieved his purpose.

Less than a week after the indictments had been returned against Townley and Gilbert in the Martin County case, Gilbert was indicted at Red Wing for violation of the Minnesota sedition act on the basis of a speech made at Kenyon, Minnesota, a full nine months earlier. It was alleged that he had said, among other things, that the United States had been "stampeded into this war by newspaper rot to pull England's chestnuts out of the fire," and that the war would end in a hurry if wealth were conscripted the same as manpower.

Gilbert and his witnesses had different versions, but the state's case was based largely on the testimony of seven witnesses, each of whom was able to repeat in identical order, word for word, the same ten sentences, admittedly not made originally in continuous fashion, from a speech delivered nine months before. Although the state's witnesses claimed not to have seen the indictments, all gave Gilbert's alleged words exactly as they were stated in that indictment. Despite this remarkable feat of memory, none of the witnesses was able to remember anything else Gilbert had said. One of these witnesses claimed to have written notes on the speech as it was being given. This was supposedly done in a notebook held on his knee and in a dimly lit hall, yet the notes were in ink and in small regular handwriting. In spite of the extremely unlikely validity of the testimony of what the *Leader* termed the "parrot chorus," it was accepted at face value.

Judge Albert Johnson had ruled at the opening of the trial that no member of the Nonpartisan League might sit on the jury, a move which the League claimed meant that only opponents would be permitted to serve, since neutrals at this time were few and far between. Later the judge had refused to permit the defense to attempt to show animus against the Nonpartisan League on the part of several of the state's witnesses, saying that "the League is not on trial." Yet when, after imposing the maximum sentence of a year in jail and a $500 fine, Judge Johnson was asked to grant the usual stay of sentence pending appeal, he proposed to make the stay conditional upon a promise that the League would refrain from all further activities in Goodhue County. This Gilbert refused to consider, and the stay was finally granted without the promise.

In December of 1918 the state Supreme Court upheld the conviction, concerning itself for the most part with the alleged errors on the part of the lower court, and the League attorneys promptly appealed to the Supreme Court of the United States, claiming that the state statute was unconstitutional as a violation of the guarantee of free speech and as being legislation within the exclusive province of the Congress. Two years later, on December 13, 1920, the majority of the Court, speaking through Mr. Justice McKenna, held that the state statute involved merely cooperation with the United States and was not in conflict with the federal law. Moreover, it was a valid exercise of the state's police power which did not violate the Fourteenth Amendment in unduly abridging free speech. "The right of free speech," said McKenna, "does not cover false and malicious misrepresentation of the objects and motives of this country in entering upon a war . . ."

Justice Holmes concurred in the result without subscribing to the majority opinion, while Chief Justice White dissented on the grounds that the subject matter was within the exclusive legislative power of the Congress, and the Congress having acted, the entire field was occupied. Mr. Justice Brandeis filed a powerful dissent, surpassing the majority opinion in both length and logic, in which he agreed with the chief justice but put his primary emphasis upon the free speech issue. The statute, he said, "aims to prevent not acts but beliefs." Free speech includes the right to teach a doctrine of pacifism and that the abolition of war is possible, "so long, at least, as Congress has not declared that the public safety demands its suppression." "I cannot believe," he concluded, "that the liberty guaranteed by the Fourteenth Amendment includes only liberty to acquire and enjoy property."

The Brandeis dissent, Chafee[2] points out, was "the first time that any member of the Court, in any kind of published opinion, squarely maintained that freedom of speech is protected against State action by the United States Constitution." The Minnesota statute, says Chafee, was the first attempt by a state to curb opposition to war since the early years of the American revolution:

It remained for our own day, when the doctrine of states' rights was supposed to be on its last legs, to establish by a Supreme Court decision . . . that the weapons which Massachusetts and Virginia used against the disloyal remain sharp and active in the hands of modern State governments and were not surrendered to the nation in 1789.

Five years after the Gilbert decision, however, the Court in *Gitlow v. New York* was ready to agree unanimously with what was essentially the position on protection of free speech, through the Fourteenth Amendment, maintained in the Brandeis dissent.

● ● ●

These months of terrorism in the League states constitute a period difficult to assess. The League always maintained that the reason for its persecution was purely political, engineered by those who either feared the end of their own political dominance or who feared the economic program to which the League was committed. It is scarcely deniable that this was a most important factor in the attitude of many high officials, persons in positions of economic power, and numerous newspapers, but it does not adequately explain the mob brutalities in hundreds of small towns. Nothing was more significant than the treatment of the League by the press, which largely determined the attitude of most persons who did not hear League speakers for themselves. Passions are easily inflamed in a war period when fear and hate are dominant. Many unthinking persons naively assumed that violence against those who, it claimed, were opposed to the war somehow demonstrated their own patriotism and superiority, and once a mob has been started on its way no one, of course, stops to reason. The possession of virtually unrestricted power by some local officials or citizens unused

[2] Zechariah Chafee, Jr., an authority on American law. [*Editor's note.*]

to such affluence often proved too great a temptation and led to abuse. Doubtless in some cases motives were mixed, but it was easy and socially acceptable to justify opposition to the League on patriotic grounds.

The desire to make a scapegoat of a minority probably also entered into the picture, a fact which is perhaps evidenced to some degree by the previously mentioned tendency for the greatest violence and bitterest opposition to appear in areas where the League was least strongly organized. The League was promoting a program which would normally have been popular with the classes they sought to interest, but its opponents were able to so emphasize the "loyalty" issue that all else was lost sight of by the average man. The popularity which it did achieve in the face of such tremendous opposition is in some ways little short of astonishing. It is worthy of note that there is scarcely a case on record of a League group reciprocating violence. It was well known what sort of publicity any such incident would receive, and the League desired always to be able to point to its membership as the peaceful and law-abiding element of society.

It is quite clear that a goodly number of League members were opposed to the war, certainly at least in the early days, and it is possible that there were some who entertained pro-German sentiments, though such a matter is difficult to prove. There may also have been members of the bankers' associations with similar feelings, but that fact alone could hardly condemn either organization. Judged on the basis of both the League's pronouncements and its actions, the charges of wartime disloyalty of the Nonpartisan League break down completely.

The war record of North Dakota, the only state with a League administration, was one of the best. Despite repeated poor crops the state oversubscribed all three Liberty Loans, the first by 140 per cent, the second by 70 per cent (the largest oversubscription of any state on this loan), and the third by 76 per cent. The record on volunteers for the armed services was excellent, while the cost per draftee in North Dakota was $1.83 as against an average of $4.23 for all other states. In the last Red Cross drive North Dakota more than doubled its allotment, and it subscribed $175,000 on an allotment for the YMCA of $100,000. In 1918 North Dakota increased its wheat acreage more than 630,000 acres at the request of the government. It was one of the first states to provide a moratorium protecting soldiers against foreclosures, and to decree that all persons between eighteen and fifty must be employed in essential occupations; it was the first to provide a soldiers' bonus.

The postwar attitude of George Creel, the wartime chairman of the National Committee on Public Information as to the loyalty of the Nonpartisan League was clearly expressed in response to an inquiry from Charles Edward Russell:

I am not at all unwilling to give you my opinion with respect to the war attitude of the Nonpartisan League. Never at any time did I consider it a disloyal organization. On the contrary, the war record of the state of North Dakota, controlled by the League, proved conclusively that the membership, taken as a whole, gave America faithful and ungrudging support in the hour of need.

There is no question, however, but that the Nonpartisan League in the beginning was poisoned by many misunderstandings. Particularly was this true in the matter of the lie that Wall Street was the cause of America's entrance, and that the war was nothing more nor less than the effort of rich men to increase and protect their profits. These beliefs, however, were not peculiar to the Nonpartisan League, but were held by great groups of workers and farmers of the Western States.

It was not a condition that should have caused any wonder. During the long period of America's neutrality, press and politicians alike were divided on the issues involved. . . .

I sent for the heads of various agricultural bodies and unions, and among those that came to Washington in response to the call was Mr. Townley . . . I found him, just as I found the others, full of distrusts and suspicions born of the many lies that he had read and heard. I took him, as I took others, to the President himself, and the interview removed every doubt as to the necessity of the war and the high purpose of America. And after that I took Mr. Townley to the office of Mr. Herbert Hoover, and for three hours the two men fought out disputed points. When Mr. Townley left Washington he had not only pledged the full support of his organization to the war, but he had struck hands with Mr. Hoover and promised every cooperative effort. These pledges were kept . . .

I am not familiar with the purposes or principles of the Nonpartisan League. For all I know they may be good or they may be bad, but what I do know is that the League itself had a better war record than that of many organizations operating in the name of a 100-per-cent patriotism . . .

Postwar Upheaval: Racism and Riots

JOHN HOPE FRANKLIN

In times of national trial, American Negroes have seldom escaped especial difficulties. Moreover, the prewar period of progressivism, so filled with change in other areas, had seen little advance in Negro rights—and much neglect or even hostility on the part of many leaders of reform. It was almost inevitable that the same spirit directed toward NPL farmers should find even more violent expression when directed toward Negroes.

The wartime experience greatly exacerbated relations between Negroes and whites. Between 1914 and 1918 about half a million Negroes migrated from the South to northern and midwestern cities in response to the demand for unskilled labor. Crowded into slums and often used as strikebreakers by employers, Negroes became the objects of the suspicion and hatred of white unskilled workers. An anti-Negro riot swept through East St. Louis, Illinois, in July, 1917. It was only a harbinger of the travail that lay ahead in the months following the Armistice. In the following excerpt, the leading historian of American Negroes has described the suffering that Negroes had to endure during the troubled time of demobilization.

From John Hope Franklin, *From Slavery to Freedom: A History of American* *Negroes,* pp. 477–486. Copyright 1947, © 1956 and 1967 by Alfred A. Knopf, Inc. Reprinted by permission of the publisher.

A LTHOUGH SOME NEGRO SOLDIERS WHO SERVED IN FRANCE WERE hesitant about making the return trip to the United States lest they lose what democracy and freedom they had found in far-away places, the great majority seemed anxious to rejoin their loved ones in their native land. Some doubtless believed that conditions would be better than before the war, while others were indifferent to the future, thinking only of the pleasures of being home again. They were not required to wait very long before finding out what changes, if any, had taken place in the United States, for shortly after the Armistice was signed the American military authorities began to make preparations for the return and demobilization of American troops. Some Negro troops were detained to assist in the tasks of cleaning up the camp sites and clearing away the debris left from the battles, but the greater part of them were en route to the United States within four months after the end of the war. By April, 1919, many Negro troops were already in the United States, and some of them were being demobilized.

Since most of the Negro troops disembarked in the New York area, their first reception in the United States was enthusiastic. New York City seemed never to tire of the apparently endless parades of troops, both black and white, that proceeded almost immediately from their ships to make the triumphal march up Fifth Avenue. When New York's own Negro regiment, the 369th, returned on February 17, 1919, approximately one million persons witnessed their parade from lower New York up through Fifth Avenue to Harlem. A similar reception was given various units of the Ninety-second Division, the last of whose troops landed at Hoboken on March 12, 1919. Other cities, however, vied with New York in welcoming their Negro troops. Buffalo turned out en masse to receive its darker brothers, while huge crowds filled the streets of St. Louis to cheer the Negroes who had fought in Europe. When the 370th, the "Old Eighth Illinois," reached Chicago, much of the business of the city was suspended to welcome the veterans. The soldiers paraded through the Loop as well as through the thickly populated Negro South Side, and in many places the crowds were so dense that the troops could not march in regular formation. If the parades were not so large and the enthusiasm not so great in the South, it could easily be attributed to the fact that no Negro units came from single communities, as well as to the fact that Southern whites did not enjoy seeing Negroes armed with powerful weapons. Few stopped to give much consideration to such a matter, however.

It was a time of jubilation, and Negroes were determined to enjoy it while it lasted.

The period of jubilation was short-lived, however, for the business of settling down to post-war living became more urgent with every passing day. Indeed, all America was anxious to put the war behind it and return to a peace-time existence. Industry was desirous of beginning its program of filling the huge backlog of orders for goods that were not produced during the war. Labor was ready to press for demands that it could not afford to make during the war, and to perfect its organization to the point where its effectiveness could not be nullified by strike-breakers. Politicians could hardly wait to get the peace treaties out of the way in order to wage a campaign in 1920 that they hoped would be free of the issues of the war. Militant Negro leaders were anxious, too. They did not want to return to a pre-war normalcy, but to move forward to a new basis for democratic living in the United States. In May, 1919, the editor of the *Crisis*[1] undertook to speak for returning Negro soldiers when he said:

We return from the slavery of uniform which the world's madness demanded us to don to the freedom of civil garb. We stand again to look America squarely in the face and call a spade a spade. We sing: This country of ours, despite all its better souls have done and dreamed, is yet a shameful land.

It *lynches*. . . . It *disfranchises* its own citizens. . . . It encourages *ignorances*. . . . It steals from us. . . . It insults us. . . .

We *return*. We *return from fighting*. We *return fighting*.

Make way for Democracy! We saved it in France, and by the Great Jehovah, we will save it in the U.S.A., or know the reason why.

The editor had not spoken too early, for if he and other Negroes were determined to secure a larger share of democracy for themselves, there were many white citizens who were as determined to see that there shall be no wholesale distribution of the blessings of liberty. Whites had steeled themselves against the day when Negro soldiers would return and make demands for first-class citizenship, and they were ready to put the machinery they had perfected into operation. The Ku Klux Klan had been revived in the Southern states as early as 1915. Its growth was slow until the end of the war, at which time it came forth with a broad program for "uniting native-born white Christians for concerted action in the preservation of American institutions and the supremacy of the white race." Within a year it grew from an impotent organization of a few thousand members to a militant

[1] William E. B. Du Bois. [*Editor's note.*]

union of more than 100,000 white-hooded knights. It declared itself against Negroes, Japanese and other orientals, Roman Catholics, Jews, and all foreign-born persons. It capitalized on the isolationist reaction that followed the war and spread into areas where previously there had been few manifestations of race hatred. It assumed the responsibility for punishing persons whom it considered dangerous to the growth of its ideas and spearheaded the drive for violence and intimidation toward Negroes. Within ten months, shortly after the close of the war, the Klan made more than 200 public appearances in 27 states. Cells of the organization flourished in several New England states, as well as in New York, Indiana, Illinois, Michigan, and other Northern and Midwestern states. Its assumption of a semi-official role, in taking the law into its own hands and in luring public servants into its membership, stimulated the lawlessness and violence that characterized the post-war period in the United States.

At a public meeting one Klansman exclaimed, "We would not rob the colored population of their rights, but we demand that they respect the rights of the white race in whose country they are permitted to reside." Actually, there were few rights of Negroes that the Klan felt obliged to respect, and it acted in a manner confirming its contention that the United States was a "white man's country." In Texas the Klan became the instrument of a new Negro enslavement, forcing Negroes to work and pick cotton at wages they would not have accepted if the decision had been left to them. Throughout the South and Southwest Negroes lived in constant fear of the hooded bands of night riders who burned crosses to terrify the non-Gentile element of the population. In the West the Klan was also active, especially against the Japanese population. Wherever it established itself it was blamed, correctly or incorrectly, for the atrocities committed in the vicinity. There were floggings, branding with acid, tarring and feathering, hangings, and burnings. The victims were largely, though not entirely, Negroes. It was a new day, indeed—a new day of violence and terror.

White citizens, in and out of the Klan, poured out a wrath upon the Negro population shortly after the war that could hardly be viewed as fit punishment even for a treasonable group of persons. More than 70 Negroes were lynched during the first year of the post-war period. Ten Negro soldiers, several still in their uniforms, were lynched. Mississippi and Georgia mobs murdered three returned soldiers each; in Arkansas two were lynched; while Florida and Alabama each took the life of a Negro soldier by mob violence. Fourteen Negroes were burned publicly, eleven of whom were burned alive. In utter despair a Negro editor of Charleston, South Carolina, cried out, "There is scarcely a day that passes that newspapers don't tell about a Negro soldier lynched in his uniform. Why do they lynch Negroes, anyhow? With a white judge, a white jury, white public sentiment, white officers of the law, it is just as impossible for a Negro accused of crime, or even suspected of crime, to escape the white man's vengeance or his justice as it would be for a fawn to escape that wanders accidentally into a den of hungry lions. So why not give him the semblance of a trial."

It was the summer of 1919, called by James Weldon Johnson "The Red Summer," that ushered in the greatest period of interracial strife the nation had ever witnessed. From June to the end of the year approximately 25 race riots were held in American urban centers. Some were large; others were small; all were indicative of a thoroughly malodorous situation in race relations. Even after the war the migration of Negroes to urban centers continued and, in some areas, increased. Jobs were not so plentiful as they had been during the war years, and competition strained the relations of whites and Negroes. Meanwhile, the high rents in the segregated residential areas continued. Unrest and disappointment seized a considerable portion of the Negro population, and when it became clear that many whites were seeking to deprive them of some of the gains they had made during the war, Negroes bristled into action and showed a willingness to defend themselves that they had not shown before. The riots were not confined to any section of the country. They were Northern and Southern, Eastern and Western—wherever whites and Negroes undertook the task of living together. Egged on by native fascist organizations like the Ku Klux Klan, the lawless element of the population undertook to terrorize the Negroes into submission.

In July, 1919, Longview, Texas, witnessed the nightmare of a race riot. Several white men were shot when they went into the Negro section of the town in search of a Negro school teacher who was accused of sending a release to the *Chicago Defender* concerning the lynching of a Negro during the previous month. Whites of the town were alarmed over this show of strength among the Negroes, and they poured into the Negro section determined to teach the Negroes a lesson. Many homes were burned, a Negro school principal was flogged on the streets, and several leading Negro citizens were run out of town. It was several days before the town returned to normalcy. In the following week a riot of more violent proportions broke out in the nation's capital. Newspaper reports of Negroes assaulting white women whipped the irresponsible elements of the population into a frenzy, although it early became clear that the reports had no basis in fact. Mobs, consisting primarily of white sailors, soldiers, and marines, ran amuck through the streets of Washington for three days, killing several Negroes and injuring scores of others. On the third day the Negroes retaliated when hoodlums sought to invade and burn the Negro section of the city. The casualty list mounted, but before order was restored the number of whites killed and wounded had increased considerably due to the belated but stern action which the Negroes took.

The most serious racial outbreak occurred in Chicago late in July of the "Red Summer." Chicago had become to the Southern Negro "the top of the world," and thousands had migrated there during and after the war in search of employment and freedom. Within less than a decade the Negro population of the city had more than doubled, and the census of 1920 showed approximately 109,000 Negroes living there. There was, of course, some friction in industry, but because of the abundance of jobs it had remained at a minimum. The most serious friction came in housing and recreation. Negroes were spreading into white neighborhoods, whereupon the whites sought to prevent it by bombing the homes of Negroes. Groups of young men took it upon themselves to frighten the Negroes into submission and to prevent their continued movement into white sections of the city. In June two Negroes were murdered, an act that ushered in a month of terror.

The riot that began on July 27 had its immediate origin in an altercation at a Lake Michigan beach. A young Negro swimming offshore had drifted into water that was customarily used by whites. White swimmers commanded him to return to his part of the beach, and some threw stones at him. When the young Negro went down and drowned, the Negroes declared that he had been murdered. Although his recovered body showed no marks of having been stoned, it was too late to save the city from a riot that was already in progress. Distorted rumors circulated among Negroes and whites concerning the incident and the subsequent events at the beach. Mobs sprang up in various parts of the city, and during the entire night there was sporadic fighting. In the next afternoon white bystanders meddled with Negroes as they went home from work. Some were pulled off street cars and whipped. Many persons of both races were injured in these clashes, and at least five were killed. On the Negro South Side a group of young Negroes stabbed an old Italian peddler to death, and a white laundry operator was also stabbed to death. During that day and the next the riot spread, with mobs of both races doing what they could to terrorize the opposite group. For thirteen days Chicago was without law and order, despite the fact that the militia was called out on the fourth day of the riot. When the authorities counted the casualties the tally sheet gave the appearance of the results of a miniature war.

Thirty-eight persons had been killed, including 15 whites and 23 Negroes; of the 537 persons injured, 178 were whites and 342 were Negroes. There is no record of the racial identity of the remaining 17. More than 1,000 families, mostly Negroes, were homeless due to the burnings and general destruction of property. It was the nation's worst race war and shocked even the most indifferent persons into a realization that interracial conflicts in the United States had reached a serious stage.

During the next two months riots occurred, among other places, in Knoxville, Tennessee, Omaha, Nebraska, and Elaine, Arkansas. The Knoxville riot was started when a white woman stumbled and killed herself while running from a Negro who was later accused of attempting to assault her. When the Negro was arrested, a mob was formed and an attempt was made to take him from the jail. During the general riot which followed scores of people were injured, some fatally, and more than $50,000 worth of property was destroyed. The troops that were called out went into the Negro section and "shot it up" when a false rumor was circulated that some Negroes had killed two white men. Negroes were stopped on the streets and searched. One man going three blocks was searched seven times. A Negro newspaper declared, "The indignities which colored women suffered at the hands of these soldiers would make the devil blush for shame."

In Omaha a mob almost completely destroyed the county courthouse by fire in order to secure a Negro who was in jail on the charge of attacking a white girl. The group succeeded in seizing the Negro, whereupon he was dragged through the streets, was shot more than a thousand times, and was mutilated beyond recognition. He was finally hanged downtown at one of the busiest intersections. Meanwhile, much damage was done to property, and several Negroes were severely beaten. Negroes in Elaine, Arkansas, met to make plans to force their landlords to make a fair settlement with them. The meeting was broken up by a deputy sheriff and a posse, and in the melee the deputy was killed. A reign of terror began in which scores of Negroes were shot and several killed. In the trials which lasted less than an hour, 12 Negro farmers were sentenced to death and 67 others were given long prison terms. The decisions were later nullified by the Supreme Court which found that the Negroes had not been given a fair trial.

Although rioting continued for the next few years, few outbreaks equaled in proportion those of 1919. Two years later, in June, 1921, the Negroes and whites of Tulsa, Oklahoma, engaged in fighting which some residents prefer to call a "race war," in which 9 whites and 21 Negroes were known to have been killed and several hundred injured. When news reached Negroes of the accusation of an assault of a young white woman by a Negro, Negroes took arms to the jail to protect the accused person, who, it was rumored, would be lynched. Altercations between whites and Negroes at the jail spread to other parts of the city, and general rioting, looting, and houseburning began. Four companies of the National Guard were called out, but by the time order was restored more than one million dollars worth of property had been destroyed or damaged. This progressive young city of the Southwest was thus added to the list of communities in which there was no interracial peace. Detroit, in 1925, joined the ranks by seeking to prevent a Negro physician, Dr. O. H. Sweet, from living in a home he had purchased in a white neighborhood. When a mob gathered around his home and threw stones, a white man was killed by gunfire coming from the house. Dr. Sweet, his brother, and his friends in the house were brought to trial. The National Association for the Advancement of Colored People came to their defense, employing Clarence Darrow and Arthur Garfield Hays as the defense attorneys. All were finally acquitted, but irreparable damage had been done not only to the Sweet family but also to race relations in Detroit.

In the post-war racial strife the Negro's willingness to fight and to die in his own defense injected a new factor into America's most perplexing social problem. It was no longer a case of one race intimidating another into submission. Now it was war in the full sense of the word, and Negroes were as determined to win it as they had been in Europe. The increasing urbanization of Negroes, with its accompanying stimulation of self-respect and racial cohesiveness, had much to do with the resistance that Negroes offered to their would-be oppressors. They had, moreover, imbibed freely of the democratic doctrine that had been expounded so generally during the war. Even if they could not win in the one-sided struggle they were carrying on, they sought to make a good showing. One of the outstanding poets of the period, Claude McKay, expressed the feelings of a great many Negroes when he wrote:

> If we must die, let it not be like hogs
> Hunted and penned in an inglorious spot,
> While round us bark the mad and hungry dogs,
> Making their mock at our accursed lot.
> If we must die, O let us nobly die,
> So that our precious blood may not be shed
> In vain; then even the monsters we defy
> Shall be constrained to honor us though dead!
> O kinsmen! we must meet the common foe!
> Though far outnumbered let us show us brave,

And for their thousand blows deal one deathblow!
What though before us lies the open grave?
Like men we'll face the murderous, cowardly pack,
Pressed to the wall, dying but fighting back!

Many whites freely intimated that it was foreign influences, especially the association on the basis of equality with the French during the war and the propaganda of Bolshevists after the war, that caused Negroes to fight back. Negroes, however, ridiculed this view and contended that they were fighting only for what they thought was right. In October, 1919, the *Pittsburgh Courier* declared, "As long as the Negro submits to lynchings, burnings, and oppressions—and says nothing he is a loyal American citizen. But when he decides that lynchings and burnings shall cease even at the cost of some bloodshed in America, then he is a Bolshevist." The militant *Crusader* regarded such accusations as a compliment. In a scathing denunciation of mob violence and rioting in America its editor asserted, "If to fight for one's rights is to be Bolshevists, then we are Bolshevists and let them make the most of it!"

Negroes loudly protested against practices which they termed injustices and oppressions. They freely admitted that democracy had escaped, despite the fact that they had pursued it with an earnestness and vigor of which few other races could boast. Disillusionment and despair settled over them, and they could express little but dejection in their utterances, which were largely directed rather indiscriminately toward the white population. After describing the burning alive of a young Negro boy in Vicksburg, Mississippi, the *Challenge Magazine* of Chicago exclaimed, "The 'German Hun' is beaten but the world is made no safer for Democracy. Humanity has been defended but lifted no higher. Democracy never will be safe in America until these occurrences are made impossible either by the execution of the law or with double barrel shot guns. . . . I hate every Hun, and the worst I know are the ones that thrive under the free institutions of America." It would take more than utterances to gain a respected place for Negroes in American life. Indeed, it became clearer that it would take more than the feverish fighting back that Negroes courageously performed in times of crisis. Intelligent planning and action were needed; but the difficulty lay in taking such steps in a climate so completely charged with emotion and tension. Small wonder that the programs for the salvation of the Negro that evolved during the period were of such varied approaches and such diverse goals.

Postwar Upheaval: The Red Scare

STANLEY COBEN

If Americans were, as Senator James A. Reed of Missouri said, suffering from "shell shock" in 1919, the trauma stemmed in part from the impact of the War, in part from the impact of postwar developments like inflation, labor unrest, the seeming threat of Bolshevism, bomb scares, and political malaise resulting from the rudderless quality of domestic politics. Stanley Coben, biographer of Attorney General A. Mitchell Palmer, who was chiefly responsible for the biggest raid against alleged radicals, describes the beginnings and development of the first American Red Scare in the following article. Colben attributes the hysteria of the Red Scare primarily to nativism, or an unreasoning fear that basic American institutions and traditions were under attack by a variety of foes. Many of his observations help to explain the anti-NPL and anti-Negro agitation described in the two preceding selections, for in a sense the alleged threat of communism was merely the most extreme of many challenges to American patterns so alarming to nativists and reactionaries.

From Stanley Coben, "A Study in Nativism: The American Red Scare of 1919–1920," *Political Science Quarterly*, LXXIX (March, 1964), 52, 59–75. Reprinted by permission of the *Political Science Quarterly*. The footnotes in the original text have been omitted.

A T A VICTORY LOAN PAGEANT IN THE DISTRICT OF COLUMBIA ON May 6, 1919, a man refused to rise for the playing of "The Star-Spangled Banner." As soon as the national anthem was completed an enraged sailor fired three shots into the unpatriotic spectator's back. When the man fell, the *Washington Post* reported, "the crowd burst into cheering and handclapping." In February of the same year, a jury in Hammond, Indiana, took two minutes to acquit the assassin of an alien who yelled, "To Hell with the United States." Early in 1920, a clothing store salesman in Waterbury, Connecticut, was sentenced to six months in jail for having remarked to a customer that Lenin was "the brainiest," or "one of the brainiest" of the world's political leaders. Dramatic episodes like these, or the better known Centralia Massacre, Palmer Raids, or May Day riots, were not everyday occurrences, even at the height of the Red Scare. But the fanatical one hundred per cent Americanism reflected by the Washington crowd, the Hammond jury, and the Waterbury judge pervaded a large part of our society between early 1919 and mid-1920.

• • •

The ferocious outbreak of nativism in the United States after World War I was not consciously planned or provoked by any individual or group, although some Americans took advantage of the movement once it started. Rather, the Red Scare . . . was brought on largely by a number of severe social and economic dislocations which threatened the national equilibrium. The full extent and the shocking effects of these disturbances of 1919 have not yet been adequately described. Runaway prices, a brief but sharp stock market crash and business depression throughout Europe, widespread fear of domestic revolt, bomb explosions, and an outpouring of radical literature were distressing enough. These sudden difficulties, moreover, served to exaggerate the disruptive effects already produced by the social and intellectual ravages of the World War and the preceding reform era, and by the arrival, before the war, of millions of new immigrants. This added stress intensified the hostility of Americans strongly antagonistic to minority groups, and brought new converts to blatant nativism from among those who ordinarily were not overtly hostile toward radicals or recent immigrants.

Citizens who joined the crusade for one hundred per cent Americanism sought, primarily, a unifying force which would halt the apparent disintegration of their culture. The movement, they felt, would eliminate those foreign influences which the one hundred per centers believed were the major cause of their anxiety.

Many of the postwar sources of stress were also present during World War I, and the Red Scare, as John Higham has observed, was partly an exaggeration of wartime passions. In 1917–18 German-Americans served as the object of almost all our nativistic fervor; they were the threatening intruders who refused to become good citizens. "They used America," a patriotic author declared in 1918 of two million German-Americans, "they never loved her. They clung to their old language, their old customs, and cared nothing for ours. . . . As a class they were clannish beyond all other races coming here." Fear of subversion by German agents was almost as extravagant in 1917–18 as anxiety about "reds" in the postwar period. Attorney General Thomas Watt Gregory reported to a friend in May 1918 that "we not infrequently receive as many as fifteen hundred letters in a single day suggesting disloyalty and the making of investigations."

Opposition to the war by radical groups helped smooth the transition among American nativists from hatred of everything German to fear of radical revolution. The two groups of enemies were associated also for other reasons. High government officials declared after the war that German leaders planned and subsidized the Bolshevik Revolution. When bombs blasted homes and public buildings in nine cities in June 1919, the director of the Justice Department's Bureau of Investigation asserted that the bombers were "connected with Russian bolshevism, aided by Hun money." In November 1919, a year after the armistice, a popular magazine warned of "the Russo-German movement that is now trying to dominate America. . . ."

Even the wartime hostility toward German-Americans, however, is more understandable when seen in the light of recent anthropological and psychological studies. World War I disturbed Americans not only because of the real threat posed by enemy armies and a foreign ideology. For many citizens it had the further effect of shattering an already weakened intellectual tradition. When the European governments decided to fight, they provided shocking evidence that man was not, as most educated members of Western society had believed, a rational creature progressing steadily, if slowly, toward control of his environment. When the great powers declared war in 1914, many Americans as well as many Europeans were stunned. The *New York Times* proclaimed a common theme—European civilization had collapsed: The supposedly advanced nations, declared the *Times,* "have reverted to the condition of savage tribes roaming the forests and falling upon each other in a fury of blood and carnage to achieve the ambitious designs of chieftains clad in skins and drunk with mead." Franz Alexander, director for twenty-five years of the Chicago Institute of Psychoanalysis, recently recalled his response to the outbreak of the World War:

> The first impact of this news is [sic] unforgettable. It was the sudden intuitive realization that a chapter of history had ended. . . . Since then, I have discussed this matter with some of my contemporaries and heard about it a great deal in my early postwar psychoanalytic treatments of patients. To my amazement, the others who went through the same events had quite a similar reaction. . . . It was an immediate vivid and prophetic realization that something irrevocable of immense importance had happened in history.

Americans were jolted by new blows to their equilibrium after entering the war. Four million men were drafted away from familiar surroundings and some of them experienced the terrible carnage of trench warfare. Great numbers of women left home to work in war industries or to replace men in other jobs. Negroes flocked to Northern industrial areas by the hundreds of thousands, and their first mass migration from the South created violent racial antagonism in Northern cities.

During the war, also, Americans sanctioned a degree of government control over the economy which deviated sharply from traditional economic individualism. Again, fears aroused before the war were aggravated, for the reform legislation of the Progressive era had tended to increase government intervention, and many citizens were further perturbed by demands that the federal government enforce even higher standards of economic and social morality. By 1919, therefore, some prewar Progressives as well as conservatives feared the gradual disappearance of highly valued individual opportunity and responsibility. Their fears were fed by strong postwar calls for continued large-scale government controls—extension of federal operation of railroads and of the Food Administration, for example.

The prime threat to these long-held individualistic values, however, and the most powerful immediate stimulus to the revitalistic response, came from Russia. There the Bolshevik conquerors proclaimed their intentions of exporting Marxist ideology. If millions of Americans were disturbed in 1919 by the specter of communism, the underlying reason was not fear of foreign invasion—Russia, after all, was still a backward nation recently badly defeated by German armies. The real threat was the potential spread of communist ideas. These, the one hundred per centers realized with horror, possessed a genuine appeal for reformers and for the economically underprivileged, and if accepted they would complete the transformation of America.

A clear picture of the Bolshevik tyranny was not yet available; therefore, as after the French Revolution, those who feared the newly successful ideology turned to fight the revolutionary ideals. So the *Saturday Evening Post* declared editorially in November 1919 that "History will see our present state of mind as one with that preceding the burning of witches, the children's crusade, the great tulip craze and other examples of softening of the world brain." The *Post* referred not to the Red Scare or the impending Palmer Raids, but to the spread of communist ideology. Its editorial concluded: "The need of the country is not more idealism, but more pragmatism; not communism, but common sense." One of the most powerful patriotic groups, the National Security League, called upon members early in 1919 to "teach 'Americanism.' This means the fighting of Bolshevism . . . by the creation of well defined National Ideals." Members "must preach Americanism and instil the idealism of America's Wars, and that American spirit of service which believes in giving as well as getting." New York attorney, author, and educator Henry Waters Taft warned a Carnegie Hall audience late in 1919 that Americans must battle "a propaganda which is tending to undermine our most cherished social and political institutions and is having the effect of producing widespread unrest among the poor and the ignorant, especially those of foreign birth."

When the war ended Americans also confronted the disturbing possibility, pointed up in 1919 by the struggle over the League of Nations, that Europe's struggles would continue to be their own. These factors combined to make the First World War a traumatic experience for millions of citizens. As Senator James Reed of Missouri observed in August 1919, "This country is still suffering from shell shock. Hardly anyone is in a normal state of mind. . . . A great storm has swept over the intellectual world and its ravages and disturbances still exist."

The wartime "shell shock" left many Americans extraordinarily susceptible to psychological stress caused by postwar social and economic turbulence. Most important for the course of the Red Scare, many of these disturbances had their greatest effect on individuals already antagonistic toward minorities. First of all, there was some real evidence of danger to the nation in 1919, and the nation provided the chief emotional support for many Americans who responded easily to charges of an alien radical menace. Violence flared throughout Europe after the war and revolt lifted radicals to power in several Eastern and Central European nations. Combined with the earlier Bolshevik triumph in

Russia these revolutions made Americans look more anxiously at radicals here. Domestic radicals encouraged these fears; they became unduly optimistic about their own chances of success and boasted openly of their coming triumph. Scores of new foreign language anarchist and Communist journals, most of them written by and for Southern and Eastern European immigrants, commenced publication, and the established radical press became more exuberant. These periodicals never tired of assuring readers in 1919 that "the United States seems to be on the verge of a revolutionary crisis." American newspapers and magazines reprinted selections from radical speeches, pamphlets, and periodicals so their readers could see what dangerous ideas were abroad in the land. Several mysterious bomb explosions and bombing attempts, reported in bold front page headlines in newspapers across the country, frightened the public in 1919. To many citizens these seemed part of an organized campaign of terror carried on by alien radicals intending to bring down the federal government. The great strikes of 1919 and early 1920 aroused similar fears.

Actually American radical organizations in 1919 were disorganized and poverty-stricken. The Communists were inept, almost without contact with American workers and not yet dominated or subsidized by Moscow. The IWW was shorn of its effective leaders, distrusted by labor, and generally declining in influence and power. Violent anarchists were isolated in a handful of tiny, unconnected local organizations. One or two of these anarchist groups probably carried out the "bomb conspiracy" of 1919; but the extent of the "conspiracy" can be judged from the fact that the bombs killed a total of two men during the year, a night watchman and one of the bomb throwers, and seriously wounded one person, a maid in the home of a Georgia senator.

Nevertheless, prophesies of national disaster abounded in 1919, even among high government officials. Secretary of State Robert Lansing confided to his diary that we were in real peril of social revolution. Attorney General A. Mitchell Palmer advised the House Appropriations Committee that "on a certain day, which we have been advised of," radicals would attempt "to rise up and destroy the Government at one fell swoop." Senator Charles Thomas of Colorado warned that "the country is on the verge of a volcanic upheaval." And Senator Miles Poindexter of Washington declared, "There is real danger that the government will fall." A West Virginia wholesaler, with offices throughout the state, informed the Justice Department in October 1919 that "there is hardly a respectable citizen of my acquaintance who does not believe that we are on the verge of armed conflict in this country." William C. McAdoo was told by a trusted friend that "Chicago, which has always been a very liberal minded place, seems to me to have gone mad on the question of the 'Reds.'"

Delegates to the Farmers National Congress in November 1919 pledged that farmers would assist the government in meeting the threat of revolution.

The slight evidence of danger from radical organizations aroused such wild fear only because Americans had already encountered other threats to cultural stability. However, the dislocations caused by the war and the menace of communism alone would not have produced such a vehement nativistic response. Other postwar challenges to the social and economic order made the crucial difference.

Of considerable importance was the skyrocketing cost of living. Retail prices more than doubled between 1914 and 1920, and the price rise began gathering momentum in the spring of 1919. During the summer of 1919 the dominant political issue in America was not the League of Nations; not even the "red menace" or the threat of a series of major strikes disturbed the public as much as did the climbing cost of living. The *Washington Post* early in August 1919 called rising prices, "the burning domestic issue. . . ." Democratic National Chairman Homer Cummings, after a trip around the country, told President Woodrow Wilson that more Americans were worried about prices than about any other public issue and that they demanded government action. When Wilson decided to address Congress on the question the Philadelphia *Public Ledger* observed that the administration had "come rather tardily to a realization of what is uppermost in the minds of the American people."

Then the wave of postwar strikes—there were 3,600 of them in 1919 involving over 4,000,000 workers—reached a climax in the fall of 1919. A national steel strike began in September and nationwide coal and rail walkouts were scheduled for November 1. Unions gained in membership and power during the war, and in 1919 labor leaders were under strong pressure to help workers catch up to or go ahead of mounting living costs. Nevertheless, influential government officials attributed the walkouts to radical activities. Early in 1919, Secretary of Labor William B. Wilson declared in a public speech that recent major strikes in Seattle, Butte, Montana, and Lawrence, Massachusetts, had been instituted by the Bolsheviks and the IWW for the sole purpose of bringing about a nationwide revolution in the United States. During the steel strike of early fall, 1919, a Senate investigating committee reported that "behind this strike there is massed a considerable element of I.W.W.'s, anarchists, revolutionists, and Russian soviets. . . ." In April 1920 the head of the Justice Department's General Intelligence Division, J. Edgar Hoover, declared in a public hearing that at least fifty per cent of the influence behind the recent series of strikes was traceable directly to Communist agents.

Furthermore, the nation suffered a sharp economic depression in late

1918 and early 1919, caused largely by sudden cancellations of war orders. Returning servicemen found it difficult to obtain jobs during this period, which coincided with the beginning of the Red Scare. The former soldiers had been uprooted from their homes and told that they were engaged in a patriotic crusade. Now they came back to find "reds" criticizing their country and threatening the government with violence, Negroes holding good jobs in the big cities, prices terribly high, and workers who had not served in the armed forces striking for higher wages. A delegate won prolonged applause from the 1919 American Legion Convention when he denounced radical aliens, exclaiming, "Now that the war is over and they are in lucrative positions while our boys haven't a job, we've got to send those scamps to hell." The major part of the mobs which invaded meeting halls of immigrant organizations and broke up radical parades, especially during the first half of 1919, was comprised of men in uniform.

A variety of other circumstances combined to add even more force to the postwar nativistic movement. Long before the new immigrants were seen as potential revolutionists they became the objects of widspread hostility. The peak of immigration from Southern and Eastern Europe occurred in the fifteen years before the war; during that period almost ten million immigrants from those areas entered the country. Before the anxious eyes of members of all classes of Americans, the newcomers crowded the cities and began to disturb the economic and social order. Even without other postwar disturbances a nativistic movement of some strength could have been predicted when the wartime solidarity against the German enemy began to wear off in 1919.

In addition, not only were the European revolutions most successful in Eastern and to a lesser extent in Southern Europe, but aliens from these areas predominated in American radical organizations. At least ninety per cent of the members of the two American Communist parties formed in 1919 were born in Eastern Europe. The anarchist groups whose literature and bombs captured the imagination of the American public in 1919 were composed almost entirely of Italian, Spanish, and Slavic aliens. Justice Department announcements and statements by politicians and the press stressed the predominance of recent immigrants in radical organizations. Smoldering prejudice against new immigrants and identification of these immigrants with European as well as American radical movements, combined with other sources of postwar stress to create one of the most frenzied and one of the most widespread nativistic movements in the nation's history.

The result, akin to the movements incited by the Chinese Boxers or the Indian Ghost Dancers, was called Americanism or one hundred per cent Americanism. Its objective was to end the apparent erosion of American values and the disintegration of American culture. By reaffirming those beliefs, customs, symbols, and traditions felt to be the foundation of our way of life, by enforcing conformity among the population, and by purging the nation of dangerous foreigners, the one hundred per centers expected to heal societal divisions and to tighten defenses against cultural change.

Panegyrics celebrating our history and institutions were delivered regularly in almost every American school, church, and public hall in 1919 and 1920. Many of these fervent addresses went far beyond the usual patriotic declarations. Audiences were usually urged to join a crusade to protect our hallowed institutions. Typical of the more moderate statements was Columbia University President Nicholas Murray Butler's insistence in April 1919 that "America will be saved, not by those who have only contempt and despite for her founders and her history, but by those who look with respect and reverence upon the great series of happenings extending from the voyage of the Mayflower. . . ."

What one historian has called "a riot of biographies of American heroes —statesmen, cowboys, and pioneers" appeared in this brief period. Immigrants as well as citizens produced many autobiographical testimonials to the superiority of American institutions. These patriotic tendencies in our literature were as short-lived as the Red Scare, and have been concealed by "debunking" biographies of folk heroes and skeptical autobiographies so common later in the nineteen-twenties. An unusual number of motion pictures about our early history were turned out immediately after the war and the reconstruction of colonial Williamsburg and of Longfellow's Wayside Inn was begun. With great fanfare, Secretary of State Lansing placed the original documents of the Constitution and the Declaration of Independence on display in January 1920, and the State Department distributed movies of this ceremony to almost every town and city in the United States. Organizations like the National Security League, the Association for Constitutional Government, the Sons and the Daughters of the American Revolution, the Colonial Dames of America, with the cooperation of the American Bar Association and many state Bar Associations, organized Constitution Day celebrations and distributed huge numbers of pamphlets on the subject throughout the country.

The American flag became a sacred symbol. Legionnaires demanded that citizens "Run the Reds out from the land whose flag they sully." Men suspected of radical leanings were forced to kiss the stars and stripes. A Brooklyn truck driver decided in June 1919 that it was unpatriotic to obey a New York City law obliging him to fly a red cloth on lumber which projected from his vehicle. Instead he used as a danger signal a small American flag. A policeman, infuriated at the sight of the stars and stripes flying from a lumber pile, arrested the driver on a charge of disorderly conduct. Despite the Brooklyn patriot's insistence that he meant no offense to the flag, he was reprimanded and fined by the court.

Recent immigrants, especially, were called upon to show evidence of real conversion. Great pressure was brought to bear upon the foreign-born to learn English and to forget their native tongues. As Senator William S. Kenyon of Iowa declared in October 1919, "The time has come to make this a one-language nation." An editorial in the *American Legion Weekly* took a further step and insisted that the one language must be called "American. Why even in Mexico they do not stand for calling the language the Spanish language."

Immigrants were also expected to adopt our customs and to snuff out remnants of Old World cultures. Genteel prewar and wartime movements to speed up assimilation took on a "frightened and feverish aspect." Welcoming members of an Americanization conference called by his department, Secretary of the Interior Franklin K. Lane exclaimed in May 1919, "You have been gathered together as crusaders in a great cause. . . . There is no other question of such importance before the American people as the solidifying and strengthening of true American sentiment." A Harvard University official told the conference that "The Americanization movement . . . gives men a new and holy religion. . . . It challenges each one of us to a renewed consecration and devotion to the welfare of the nation." The National Security League boasted, in 1919, of establishing one thousand study groups to teach teachers how to inculcate "Americanism" in their foreign-born students. A critic of the prevailing mood protested against "one of our best advertised American mottoes, 'One country, one language, one flag,' " which, he complained, had become the basis for a fervent nationwide program.

As the postwar movement for one hundred per cent Americanism gathered momentum, the deportation of alien non-conformists became increasingly its most compelling objective. Asked to suggest a remedy for the nationwide upsurge in radical activity, the Mayor of Gary, Indiana, replied, "Deportation is the answer, deportation of these leaders who talk treason in America and deportation of those who agree with them and work with them." "We must remake America," a popular author averred, "We must purify the source of America's population and keep it pure. . . . We must insist that there shall be an American loyalty, brooking no amendment or qualification." As Higham noted, "In 1919, the clamor of 100 per centers for applying deportation as a purgative arose to an hysterical howl. . . . Through repression and deportation on the one hand and speedy total assimilation on the other, 100 per centers hoped to eradicate discontent and purify the nation."

Politicians quickly sensed the possibilities of the popular frenzy for

Americanism. Mayor Ole Hanson of Seattle, Governor Calvin Coolidge of Massachusetts, and General Leonard Wood became the early heroes of the movement. The man in the best political position to take advantage of the popular feeling, however, was Attorney General A. Mitchell Palmer. In 1919, especially after the President's physical collapse, only Palmer had the authority, staff, and money necessary to arrest and deport huge numbers of radical aliens. The most virulent phase of the movement for one hundred per cent Americanism came early in 1920, when Palmer's agents rounded up for deportation over six thousand aliens and prepared to arrest thousands more suspected of membership in radical organizations. Most of these aliens were taken without warrants, many were detained for unjustifiably long periods of time, and some suffered incredible hardships. Almost all, however, were eventually released.

After Palmer decided that he could ride the postwar fears into the presidency, he set out calculatingly to become the symbol of one hundred per cent Americanism. The Palmer raids, his anti-labor activities, and his frequent pious professions of patriotism during the campaign were all part of this effort. Palmer was introduced by a political associate to the Democratic party's annual Jackson Day dinner in January 1920 as "an American whose Americanism cannot be misunderstood." In a speech delivered in Georgia shortly before the primary election (in which Palmer won control of the state's delegation to the Democratic National Convention), the Attorney General asserted: "I am myself an American and I love to preach my doctrine before undiluted one hundred per cent Americans, because my platform is, in a word, undiluted Americanism and undying loyalty to the republic." The same theme dominated the address made by Palmer's old friend, John H. Bigelow of Hazleton, Pennsylvania, when he placed Palmer's name in nomination at the 1920 National Convention. Proclaimed Bigelow: "No party could survive today that did not write into its platform the magic word 'Americanism.' . . . The Attorney-General of the United States has not merely professed, but he has proved his true Americanism. . . . Behind him I see a solid phalanx of true Americanism that knows no divided allegiance."

Unfortunately for political candidates like Palmer and Wood, most of the social and economic disturbances which had activated the movement they sought to lead gradually disappeared during the first half of 1920. The European revolutions were put down; by 1920 communism seemed to have been isolated in Russia. Bombings ceased abruptly after June 1919, and fear of new outrages gradually abated. Prices of food and clothing began to recede during the spring. Labor strife almost vanished from our major industries after a brief railroad walkout in April. Prosperity returned after mid-1919 and by early 1920 business activity and employment levels exceeded their wartime peaks. At the same time, it became clear that the Senate would not pass Wilson's peace treaty and that America was free to turn its back on the responsibilities of world leadership. The problems associated with the new immigrants remained; so did the disillusionment with Europe and with many old intellectual ideals. Nativism did not disappear from the American scene; but the frenzied attempt to revitalize the culture did peter out in 1920. The handful of unintimidated men, especially Assistant Secretary of Labor Louis F. Post, who had used the safeguards provided by American law to protect many victims of the Red Scare, found increasing public support. On the other hand, politicians like Palmer, Wood, and Hanson were left high and dry, proclaiming the need for one hundred per cent Americanism to an audience which no longer urgently cared.

It is ironic that in 1920 the Russian leaders of the Comintern finally took charge of the American Communist movement, provided funds and leadership, and ordered the Communist factions to unite and participate actively in labor organizations and strikes. These facts were reported in the American press. Thus a potentially serious foreign threat to national security appeared just as the Red Scare evaporated, providing a final illustration of the fact that the frenzied one hundred per centers of 1919–20 were affected less by the "red menace" than by a series of social and economic dislocations.

Although the Red Scare died out in 1920, its effects lingered. Hostility toward immigrants, mobilized in 1919–20, remained strong enough to force congressional passage of restrictive immigration laws. Some of the die-hard one hundred per centers found a temporary home in the Ku Klux Klan until that organization withered away during the mid-twenties. As its most lasting accomplishments, the movement for one hundred per cent Americanism fostered a spirit of conformity in the country, a satisfaction with the *status quo,* and the equation of reform ideologies with foreign enemies. Revitalization movements have helped many societies adapt successfully to new conditions. The movement associated with the American Red Scare, however, had no such effect. True, it unified the culture against the threats faced in 1919–20; but the basic problems—a damaged value system, an unrestrained business cycle, a hostile Russia, and communism— were left for future generations of Americans to deal with in their own fashion.

Wilsonian Liberalism, the German Problem, and the League of Nations

N. GORDON LEVIN, JR.

Woodrow Wilson was not only at the center of the world stage but was also the commanding actor on that stage when representatives of the victorious powers gathered in Paris in 1919 to prepare a world settlement. By this time Wilson was the hope of liberals who wanted a peace of reconciliation and a new order based upon open diplomacy, disarmament, the self-determination of subject and minority peoples, and an international organization to preserve the future peace. Torn between a desire to see Germany justly punished for her aggressions and the realization that only a "peace without victory" (to use Wilson's own phrase) could endure, the American President made a number of concessions to the Allies on matters of reparations, territorial and colonial claims, and the like. In the following excerpt, N. Gordon Levin, Jr., brilliantly analyzes Wilson's dilemma. He also shows how Wilson was able to resolve to his own satisfaction, if not to that of many of his liberal followers, this dilemma by the creation of the League of Nations. Wilson was confident that this agency under

From N. Gordon Levin, Jr., *Woodrow Wilson and World Politics: America's Response to War and Revolution*, pp. 161–182. Copyright © 1968 by Oxford University Press, Inc. Reprinted by permission. The footnotes in the original text have been omitted.

redemptive American leadership could bring Germany back into the family of nations and afford the vehicle for democratic collective security in the future.

U P TO THIS POINT IN OUR DISCUSSION, WE HAVE CHOSEN, FOR AN-alytic purposes, to treat separately the Wilsonian reintegrationist and punitive approaches toward Germany at Paris. By way of con-clusion, however, it is important to attempt to speak of Wilsonian policy at the Paris Peace Conference in more comprehensive terms capable of sub-suming the reintegrationist-punitive dialectic into a larger analytic syn-thesis. Ultimately we shall see that, for Wilson himself, the League of Nations served the function of resolving whatever contradictions were in-herent in his efforts to create a European settlement which would control and punish Germany and which would, at the same time, also insure against war or revolution.

On the eve of the Peace Conference, there were some serious misconcep-tions in Europe and America as to the probable nature of Wilson's role in postwar world politics. Perhaps most indicative of this situation is the fact that in late 1918 and early 1919 some European political elements expected the President to play an openly radical, if non-Bolshevik, role in European politics. Hopes for some form of open radical solidarity with Wilson against the Entente Establishment were shared by the majority of Europe's social democrats who often found themselves torn between liberal and rev-olutionary anti-imperialism. Moreover, the Allied governments and the Re-publican opposition in the United States were concerned in late 1918 that the presence of the President in Europe, which would make direct contact between Wilson and the people probable, might lead to just such an overt Wilsonian-radical union against an extremist peace. Yet such radical hopes and conservative fears proved largely groundless, because they were based on an underestimation of the extent to which Wilsonians, for all their mis-sionary American opposition to Old World imperialism, still remained fundamentally committed to the non-revolutionary politics of centrist liber-alism, to the accepted practices of international relations, and to inter-Allied unity against a defeated Germany. Let us turn then, to a more detailed analysis of the reasons behind Wilson's failure to satisfy his would-be allies among the non-Bolshevik European Left.

Part of the problem was that Wilson's supporters on the postwar Left seriously underestimated the extent to which the President and his advisers conceived of the Peace Conference in somewhat conventional terms, as a gathering of victorious Allies meeting to impose just but severe terms on a defeated criminal enemy. Social democratic hopes notwithstanding, Wilson was extremely reluctant at Paris ever to risk either inter-Allied unity or Entente political and military control of Germany in the process of attempting to check Allied extremism. Many European and American non-revolutionary radicals who hoped that Wilson would use the Peace Conference as a forum from which to launch an anti-imperialist assault on the Allies, failed to comprehend that much of the President's crusading liberalism remained, even in the postwar period, directed primarily at German imperialism in particular rather than at European imperialism in general. Indeed, it is possible, after understanding Wilson's ambivalent attitude toward the German Revolution, to describe the President's reintegrationist critique of Allied extremism operationally as an effort to moderate an essentially punitive peace. In sum, then, the non-Bolshevik radical vision of postwar democratic-socialist solidarity between Wilson, the German revolutionaries, and the Allied Left against both Allied and German imperialism was checked in part by the fact that Wilson ultimately chose moderated Allied military and political power, and not some form of social-democratic solidarity, as his prime response to the threat of German imperialism.

Yet it must also be clear from what has just been said that, in the maintenance of his reluctance to play a more openly radical role at Paris in opposition to Allied extremism, Wilson's own commitment to the reformist politics of ordered liberalism was as important an element as was his punitive orientation toward Germany. It should be noted that Wilson had, as an historian, looked favorably on Edmund Burke's opposition to the French Revolution, and that the President had interpreted Burke's position as one based on progressive liberal pragmatism and oriented toward "a sober, provident, and ordered progress in affairs." Probably it was in an address delivered before the International Law Society at Paris in the spring of 1919 that the President best expressed both his deeply felt opposition to any form of socio-political radicalism and his sense of the tension implicit in the role of the moderate reformer who seeks to contain utopian impulses within the framework of international liberal legality:

May I say that one of the things that has disturbed me in recent months is the unqualified hope that men have entertained everywhere of immediate emancipation from the things that have hampered and oppressed them. You cannot in human experience rush into the light. You have to go through the twilight into the broadening day before the noon comes and the full sun is on the landscape; and we must see to it that those who hope are not disappointed, by showing them the processes by which that hope must be realized—processes of law, processes of slow disentanglement from the many things that have bound us in the past. You cannot throw off the habits of society immediately any more than you can throw off the habits of the individual immediately. They must be slowly got rid of, or, rather, they must be slowly altered. They must be slowly adapted, they must be slowly shaped to the new ends for which we would use them. This is the process of law, if law is intelligently conceived.

The past must be overcome, but by an evolutionary rather than a revolutionary process. In the postwar period, then, Wilson did not hesitate to support the moderate politics of the anti-imperialism of liberal order against both the passions of Jacobin-like Bolsheviks and the class-oriented politics of Europe's social democrats.

There is no doubt that Wilson was anxious to avoid playing an inflammatory role in the tense class politics of postwar Europe. Especially significant here is the evidence that at Paris Wilson put his confidence in the strongly anti-socialist A.F. of L. leader Samuel Gompers as against the democratic-socialists of Europe who sought a basis of more radical solidarity with Wilsonians. Indeed, Wilson had been informed before Gompers left America that the French and British governments desired Gompers in Europe during the Peace Conference to act as a "steadying influence" on restive labor and socialist elements in the Allied countries. Nor was Lansing any more anxious than the President to exacerbate European class tensions on behalf of Wilsonian liberal goals. Of specific interest in this connection is Lansing's concern in November 1918 over the fact that the French Socialists were constantly espousing Wilson's policies. This concern reflected not only Lansing's desire clearly to separate Wilsonianism from all forms of socialist anti-imperialism, but also the Secretary's fear that the growth of radicalism was leading to the supplanting of the nation-state by the class as the basic unit in the political structure of the world. Writing to Wilson in the fall of 1918 to oppose William Bullitt's suggestion that the United States urge Allied leaders to isolate Bolshevik tendencies through a policy of co-operation with the moderate Left, Lansing argued that:

While there is a certain force in the reasoning as to peril from extreme radicalism under the leadership of such men as Liebknecht and the Independent Socialists, who affiliate with the Bolsheviks, the danger of compromise with any form of radicalism and the unwisdom of giving special recognition to a particular class of society as if it possessed exceptional rights impress me as strong reasons for rejecting such a proposal. Kerensky's experience in compromise and the results which have followed the exaltation of class at the expense of the rest of society, (whether the class be aristocratic, land owning or labor) are not encouraging to adopting the course suggested.

While there is no reply from Wilson to Lansing's letter on record, other evidence shows that the President shared the Secretary's reluctance to give any special recognition to socialist or working class politics in the postwar period.

As for Colonel House, it is true both that he did not share Lansing's negative attitude toward the non-Bolshevik Left and that during the war the Colonel once even fantasized on his own possible role at a future peace conference as a socialist suddenly rallying the world's peoples against the secret machinations of Old World diplomats. Yet, in practice at Paris, House proved as reluctant as Lansing to counsel the President to run the risk of a direct appeal to Europe's moderate radicals over the heads of established governments. Essentially, House favored a policy of behind-the-scenes contacts between the Administration and the non-Bolshevik Left in the hopes of harnessing moderately radical elements to the Wilsonian cause on the carefully controlled terms of the anti-imperialism of liberal order. Whatever their desires to oppose Allied imperialism at Paris, Wilsonians were not prepared to abandon the politics of liberal legitimacy and international decorum for any type of class-oriented radical anti-imperialism.

It is true, of course, that Wilson was very much in favor of including a provision in the League of Nations Covenant that would seek to raise the general standards of labor's working conditions on a worldwide basis. Yet it should be noted that the President did not conceive of such a labor "Magna Carta" in the League Covenant in anything approaching class-conscious or radical terms. Rather, Wilson appears to have hoped that the provision would help to curb worldwide labor unrest by reproducing, on a global scale, the same type of non-radical and progressive labor-management co-operation which the Administration saw as the answer to America's own industrial unrest. In an address delivered at Tacoma, Washington, on September 13, 1919, the President articulated this vision of a progressive liberal society in which the differences between labor and management were resolved in a larger harmony based on the public interest:

I call you to witness, my fellow citizens, that our present civilization is not satisfactory. It is an industrial civilization, and at the heart of it is an antagonism between those who labor with their hands and those who direct labor. You cannot compose those differences in the midst of war, and you cannot advance civilization unless you have a peace of which you make the peaceful and healing use of bringing these elements of civilization together into a common partnership, in which every man will have the same interest in the work of his community that those have who direct the work of the community. We have got to have leisure and freedom of mind to settle these things. This was a war against autocracy; and if you have disorder, if you have disquieted populations, if you have insurgent elements in your population, you are going to have autocracy, because the strongest is going to seize the power, as it has seized it in Russia. I want to declare that I am an enemy of the rulership of any minority, however constituted. Minorities have often been right and majorities wrong, but minorities cease to be right when they use the wrong means to make their opinions prevail. We must have peaceful means; we must have discussion.

Clearly, then, Wilson's basic tendency was to avoid class-oriented radicalism, and to search instead for ways to unite workers and capitalists in a liberal and co-operative framework of classless majoritarian consensus.

An analysis of the President's speeches delivered in Europe reveals both that Wilson remained loyal to his liberal progressive ideology of class harmony, and that he avoided direct appeals, on anything approaching class lines, to workers and socialists on behalf of his international program. The President often spoke directly to public audiences in Europe, during late 1918 and early 1919, but he invariably spoke in such a manner as to blur the more radical potentialities latent in his very presence. Wilson's references were usually to such diffuse entities as "world opinion," "humanity," "people," "great moral tide," "the conscience of the world," "voice of humanity," "mankind," "liberal men everywhere," and "the heart of the world," accompanied by no real attempt to root the support for his postwar program more concretely in the democratic-socialist movement of Europe. Moreover, the central message conveyed by many of Wilson's European speeches—to the effect that the Allied statesmen were prepared to follow the lead of their liberal peoples and to construct a forward-looking peace along popular lines—was calculated more to assuage than to exacerbate whatever radical potential for class conflict may have been latent in the contact between Wilsonian anti-imperialism and the more radicalized social groups of postwar Europe. As we shall now see, the League of Nations concept also expressed the general tendency of Wilsonian reformist ideology to remain fixed between the orthodox positions of classless liberal-nationalism and classless liberal-internationalism, while eschewing any affirmative approach toward national or international class conflict. In other words, the League gave Wilson a way to buttress further his confidence in the inseparable connection between a classless American liberal-nationalism and an international liberal order safe from socialist revolution.

Since he was unwilling to risk either the control of Germany or world liberal order by openly moving toward solidarity with the non-Bolshevik Left in opposition to German and/or Allied imperialism at Paris, Wilson was forced to devise another policy for the defense of his international goals. The President needed a moderately reformist program which would oppose both traditional imperialism and revolutionary-socialism, while remaining well grounded in the twin legitimacies of a liberal-capitalist nation-state system and of Allied-American dominance over Germany. Somehow a program would have to be devised which, while permitting

Germany to be punished and controlled, would nonetheless retain enough reintegrationist features to assure the gradual reabsorption of Germany into a viable non-Bolshevik world of liberal order. Moreover, such a program would also have to be able to legitimize ideologically the co-opting of American power into the maintenance of a basically anti-German peace settlement, by providing a liberal vision going beyond mere punitive right-eousness. Such a program would have to hold out the promise that America's complete involvement in world politics represented not a destruction of America's liberal-exceptionalism, but rather the possibility of restructuring world politics, under the inspiration of America's liberal idealism, into a new international order safe from imperialist war and from socialist revolution. Ultimately such a program was available to Wilsonians in the form of the League of Nations. It will be important, therefore, to turn now to an analysis of the Wilsonian conception of the League of Nations, in order to understand how, for the President, the League seemed to resolve all the contradictions latent in his policies at the Paris Peace Conference.

The League of Nations issue is perhaps best viewed as an institutional and ideological microcosm containing all the tensions present in the post-war Wilsonian approach to the German question. On one level of analysis, therefore, it could be argued that, along with whatever more purely reintegrationist tendencies it certainly contained, Wilson's attitude toward the League also included his related but somewhat contradictory desire to punish and to control the defeated Germans. In his major address of September 27, 1918, Wilson made it clear that, for him, one of the essential functions of a projected League of Nations would be to enforce just peace terms on a probationary Germany:

If it be in deed and in truth the common object of the Governments associated against Germany and of the nations whom they govern, as I believe it to be, to achieve by the coming settlements a secure and lasting peace, it will be necessary that all who sit down at the peace table shall come ready and willing to pay the price, the only price, that will procure it; and ready and willing, also, to create in some virile fashion the only instrumentality by which it can be made certain that the agreements of the peace will be honored and fulfilled. That price is impartial justice in every item of the settlement, no matter whose interest is crossed; and not only impartial justice, but also the satisfaction of the several peoples whose fortunes are dealt with. That indispensable instrumentality is a League of Nations formed under covenants that will be efficacious. Without such an instrumentality, by which the peace of the world can be guaranteed, peace will rest in part upon the word of outlaws and only upon that word. For Germany will have to redeem her character, not by what happens at the peace table, but by what follows.

In this connection, it is important to note that Wilson often made clear his belief that Germany ought to be excluded from the League of Nations, for a probationary period, while the Allied democracies made certain that Germany's autocratic political structure and imperialistic foreign policy had both been sufficiently liberalized. Moreover, it is also significant that on many occasions during 1919, the President spoke of the League's important role in guarding Poland and the other newly liberated states of Eastern Europe against any future economic or political aggression from Germany. Then, too, reflecting the interrelatedness of punitive and reintegrationist tendencies among Wilsonians at Paris, it is worth noting that, while Colonel House and General Bliss were more prepared than Wilson to admit Germany to the League immediately, both House and Bliss also saw the League, in part, as a device for controlling Germany.

Wilson and House also argued on occasion that the League of Nations could serve specifically as a defense for France against the threat of another German attack. Indeed, without some emphasis on the League as an anti-German bulwark, it is doubtful that Wilsonians would have been as successful as they were in moderating some of France's most extreme postwar designs on Germany. In a letter responding to Elihu Root's measured opposition to possible American over-involvement in European politics, David Hunter Miller, the Wilsonian expert on international law at Paris, succinctly conveyed his awareness of the real necessity of assuring France of America's commitment to the League of Nations, as an instrument of security against German aggression, in order to win French approval of more moderate peace terms:

> The question discussed is not only one of the highest political importance but of immediate importance. France does not think that our interest in a future attack of Germany on France is secondary but primary, and feels that that possibility should be the first concern of the world in general and of America in particular, while admitting that no such attack for the next few years is possible. Whether this feeling on the part of France is right or wrong is not the question, for it exists in a degree which it is almost impossible to overstate, and any attempt to limit our responsibility in the matter would defeat the whole Covenant, for France would prefer then to make a different kind of peace with Germany and not to have a League. Certainly without the League we could hardly refuse her the right to make a peace with Germany which would let her feel secure, but such a peace would then be made as would be contrary to everything we have stood for.

David Hunter Miller's analysis of the anti-German security aspects implicit in the League as it emerged at Paris points up for us anew one of the central paradoxes of Wilsonian policy at the Peace Conference. In its efforts to check Allied extremism and to provide for the reintegration of a liberalized Germany into a new non-revolutionary world order, the Wilson Administration was partly inhibited by the fact that the President, and many of his advisers, retained a punitive and a suspicious orientation toward the postwar German polity. Yet, even when they did disagree on German questions with the British and French, Wilsonians were also inhibited from more direct conflict with the Allies by the fear that an overt U.S.-Entente break might somehow give encouragement to manifest and latent revolutionary-socialist tendencies in postwar Europe. It followed, that to whatever extent the President and his advisers did choose to oppose Allied, and especially French, extremism at Paris, the Americans were not prepared to rely on the tactic of radical mass mobilization against imperialism. Instead, Wilsonians sought to moderate Allied policies behind the scenes by the implicit and explicit use of America's one viable weapon: namely the threat of the, possible withdrawal of the economic, political, and military power of the United States from the immense task of guaranteeing the final European settlement. It must be noted, however, that, paradoxically, the employment of such tactics meant that every concession on the German question which the Administration won in negotiation with the Entente only served to bind American power more securely to the task of guaranteeing the peace settlement. The willingness of Wilson and House, despite the reintegrationist objections of Lansing, White, and Bliss, to join Great Britain and France in a special anti-German security treaty in return for French concessions to moderation in Rhineland negotiations was the classic case in point. In sum, then, part of the American conception of the League of Nations involved anti-German security considerations.

For their own part, unlike Wilson and his advisers, the postwar leaders of France saw the League only as a *de facto* military alliance to protect France from Germany. The French would accept moderation of their demands in the Rhineland only after the United States and Great Britain agreed to sign a special security treaty guaranteeing France against unprovoked German aggression. Thus, so deeply interrelated at Paris were the Wilsonian reintegrationist and primitive orientations toward Germany that, whatever the inherent tension between them, both these approaches often coexisted in the Wilsonian response to such issues as the reparations tangle and the question of the League and French security.

In any event, there is no doubt that on one level Wilsonians were definitely prepared to conceive of the League partly as an instrument for enforcing the final peace terms on Germany, notwithstanding whatever inherent contradiction such a view might involve for the Administration's equally strong desire to reintegrate a democratized Germany into a non-revolutionary liberal-capitalist world order. In this sense, the Wilsonian orientation toward the League tended to merge well with the world views of such leading British statesmen as Lloyd George, who envisioned the absorption of American power permanently into the maintenance of a peace settlement in Europe which would fuse punitive and reintegrationist features in an uneasy balance. It is also interesting to observe that, during 1919, many security-conscious elements of the French Center and Right moved from opposition to later support of the President, as it became clear that he meant to pledge American power to the protection of France and to the maintenance of the severe peace settlement through the League of Nations and the related security treaty.

Yet if, during 1919, the French and British leaders moved to support Wilson and the League, it is true that, conversely, Europe's democratic-socialists and Left-liberals tended to move from initial support of the President to an increased rejection of Wilsonian policies. Desperate in their search of a way to end imperialism without socialist revolution, many democratic-socialists hoped that Wilson would create a League which, rather than being made up exclusively of the representatives of various foreign offices, would instead reflect the diversity of class and party interests in each member country, and would, thereby, provide a world forum capable both of being strongly influenced by socialist values and of transcending the nation-state system of world politics. However, having underestimated Wilson's loyalty to liberal-nationalist legitimacy, his distaste for any form of socialist politics, and his desire to control Germany by reliance on Allied armed power rather than through more radical means, the democratic-socialists were necessarily disillusioned by the actual League of Nations, which emerged as a union of governments implicitly pledged, in part, to enforce an anti-German peace. Radicals could see clearly that, far from ending such contradictions in world politics as the German question by any sort of revolutionary transformation, the League created by the statesmen at Paris was itself partially based on those very contradictions.

Within the Wilsonian delegation itself, at Paris, a critical approach toward the postwar Allied-American political agreements also devolped among such ardent reintegrationists as Lansing, Bliss, White, and Hoover. Convinced of the necessity strongly to oppose the Allies in the interests of a moderate settlement which would strengthen Germany as a bastion of liberal political and economic stability, these committed reintegrationists were often fearful that, in secret negotiations, House and Wilson would allow American power to be absorbed fully by the Allies into the maintenance of a severely anti-German peace capable of producing war or social revolution. Lansing, for one, even went so far as to be deeply critical of the League of Nations, which he saw as basically an alliance of the victorious powers formed primarily to enforce harsh peace terms on Germany. Lansing had envisioned instead a League with no real powers of enforcement which, by immediately including a liberalized Germany and by bringing all nations to pledge allegiance to the principles of liberal-internationalism on an equalitarian basis, could not have implicitly become a postwar extension of the Entente alliance. In part, then, Lansing, Hoover, and Bliss became somewhat "isolationist" in their reactions to events at Paris, in that they sought to keep America free from entangling economic and political ties to the Allies. Yet, their "isolationism" was always ambivalent at best, since these ardent reintegrationists also hoped, in their own way, to make possible, under the guidance of a liberal-exceptionalist America uncontaminated by power politics, the creation of a more inclusive international system of political and economic liberalism, safe from either traditional imperialism or Bolshevism.

It is true that at Paris neither Wilson nor House was indifferent either to general reintegrationist criticism of Allied policy or to the desire of the most committed American reintegrationists to defend America's political and economic freedom against possible Allied absorption. At the same time, and to a greater extent than Lansing, Bliss or White, both Wilson and House were also prepared to view the League as a device making possible the involvement of American power in the tasks of controlling Germany and of enforcing the peace settlement. Indeed, Wilson's defense of the League Covenant in America during the summer and early fall of 1919 was partly based on the argument that the League was needed to maintain American-Allied unity in the face of a Germany which had come fered severe but just punishment. This apparent contradiction could be wholly resolved in the realm of ideology, if not so completely in the area of practice, since both House and the President also saw the League of Nations as having strong counterbalancing reintegrationist potentialities.

Along with their more static vision of the League as a defender of the Versailles settlement, both the President and Colonel House also saw the League as a potentially flexible instrument through which the imperfect decisions made at Paris could be readjusted in the future. Unwilling completely to share the view of such reintegrationist critics as Lansing, Wilson and House preferred to view the League more broadly and hopefully as a living liberal institution capable of constant adaptation and growth. "A living thing is born," said Wilson of the League at one point, "and we must see to it that the clothes we put on it do not hamper it—a vehicle of power, but a vehicle in which power may be varied at the discretion of those who exercise it and in accordance with the changing circumstances of the times." Similarly, the President hoped that America's postwar participation in the work of the Reparations Commission would make possible a rational readjustment of the problematic reparations settlement which Wilsonians had been forced to accept at Paris. For Wilson, then, the League was the means of extending to the world scene an American vision of pragmatic and progressive change within the confines of a liberal order.

In this general context it is of interest to note that even such ardent reintegrationists and critics of the Paris settlement as Hoover, Lansing, Bliss, and White were in no sense immune to the notion that the League might prove to be useful in an imperfect world, by assuring some degree of continued international cooperation in the interests of world stability. Lansing's memoirs make clear that, for him, his eventual support of the cause of treaty ratification represented no change of heart from his critical stance at Paris, but rather a sense that American ratification of the Treaty and the League Covenant was necessary to the prevention of social chaos:

My own position was paradoxical. I was opposed to the Treaty, but signed it and favored its ratification. The explanation is this: Convinced after conversations with the President in July and August, 1919, that he would not consent to any effective reservations, the politic course seemed to be to endeavor to secure ratification without reservations. It appeared to be the only possible way of obtaining that for which all the world longed and which in the months succeeding the signature appeared absolutely essential to prevent the widespread disaster resulting from political and economic chaos which seemed to threaten many nations if not civilization itself. Even if the Treaty was bad in certain provisions, so long as the President remained inflexible and insistent, its ratification without change seemed a duty to humanity.

It is quite probable that, considering his general world view, Lansing had Bolshevism in mind when he referred to a "widespread disaster resulting from political and economic chaos which seemed to threaten many nations if not civilization itself." Ironically, Colonel House, a man whose constant efforts to compromise with the Allies had drawn Lansing's wrath at Paris, had been himself moved to compromise in the interests of a speedy peace partly because of a fear that Bolshevism was growing in the atmosphere of postwar uncertainty. In any event, it could be said that, in the aftermath of the Paris Peace Conference, the differences between Wilson and such reintegrationist critics within the Administration as Hoover and Lansing tended to be submerged in a unified Wilsonian effort to attain both Treaty ratification and the maintenance of world liberal-capitalist stability in the face of intransigent criticism of the Versailles Peace from the Left and the Right in the United States.

In the realm of ideology, Wilson's reintegrationist conception of the League was more powerful than his somewhat contradictory vision of the League as a means for controlling Germany and enforcing the peace settlement. After all, the President did feel that Germany would be admitted to the League after having proved her liberal sincerity, and that Germany's eventual admittance could help to ease certain problems latent in the terms of the Treaty. On September 13, 1919, Wilson clearly affirmed his idea of the future reintegration, after a period of probation, of a truly liberalized Germany:

I read you these figures in order to emphasize and set in a higher light, if I may, the substitute which is offered to us, the substitute for war, the substitute for turmoil, the substitute for sorrow and despair. That substitute is offered in the Covenant of the League of Nations. America alone cannot underwrite civilization. All the great free peoples of the world must underwrite it, and only the free peoples of the world can join the League of Nations. The membership is open only to self-governing nations. Germany is for the present excluded, because she must prove that she has changed the processes of her constitution and the purposes of her policy; but when she has proved these things she can become one of the partners in guaranteeing that civilization shall not suffer again the intolerable thing she attempted.

Thus, Wilson's conception of the League as an inter-Allied instrument to control a justly punished Germany was ultimately transcended by the President's related but broader vision of the League of Nations as an inclusive concert of liberal powers into which a reformed Germany could eventually be reintegrated.

As early as spring 1918 the President had urged that the League ought not to be "an alliance or a group formed to maintain any sort of balance of power, but must be an association which any nation is at liberty to join which is willing to cooperate in its objects and qualify in respect of its guarantees." Similarly, at Paris, Wilson affirmed that "there must now be, not a balance of power, not one powerful group of nations set off against another, but a single overwhelming, powerful group of nations who shall be the trustee of the peace of the world." Of course, it is clear that, for a time, the powerful trustees would be the victorious Allied powers, but it is significant, as Colonel House made plain, that one of the reasons for America's rejection of the French plan for an official League army was the Wilsonian concern lest the French succeed in turning the League completely into an anti-German instrument. In sum, then, the basic Wilsonian reintegrationist conception of the League, as an inclusive community of liberal states mutually pledged to defend international law and one another's territorial integrity, had the potential of ideologically transcending the actual anti-German context from within which the League emerged at Paris.

At one point, while in England late in 1918, the President spoke of the

League in terms which contained many of the ambiguities already discussed:

> I wish that it were possible for us to do something like some of my very stern ancestors did, for among my ancestors are those very determined persons who were known as the Covenanters. I wish we could, not only for Great Britain and the United States, but for France and Italy and the world, enter into a great league and covenant, declaring ourselves, first of all, friends of mankind and uniting ourselves together for the maintenance and the triumph of right.

On the one hand, both the direct mention of the Allied powers as forming the moral core of the League, and the reference to stern convenanted unity in "the maintenance and the triumph of right," could imply the creation of a League simply to defend a righteously punitive settlement against Germany. On the other hand, however, such phrases as "and the world" and "friends of mankind" obviously suggest the more inclusive and reintegrationist possibilities of Wilsonian liberal-internationalism.

There can be no doubt that the President saw the League of Nations, in part, as a postwar inter-Allied police force growing naturally out of the progressive nucleus of the Allied-American liberal alliance which had defeated the special reactionary challenge to world liberalism posed by German autocratic imperialism. Yet, beyond the necessary defeat of atavistic German imperialism, there also existed the larger Wilsonian hope to so reorganize world politics as to prevent any other nation from repeating Germany's imperialistic actions in the future. In his defense of the Versailles settlement, the President was concerned not only with reforming and controlling Imperial Germany; he also sought to liberalize the entire imperialistic system of European politics within which an autocratic Germany had simply played the most militant and aggressive single role. The President often combined an argument to the effect that the League was the necessary culmination to the triumph of world liberalism over German imperialism with a broader argument that the League was also the means by which world liberalism would finally reform the Old World's traditional balance-of-power system.

The point is that, speaking theoretically, Germany's eventual reintegration was latent in the Wilsonian critique of the traditional imperialistic system. Had Wilson joined the French in merely seeking to punish and to control German imperialism alone, the League of Nations would have been only a postwar extension of the Entente alliance. To be sure, the League was, in part, just such a peacetime extension of the anti-German wartime alliance, yet the Wilsonian critique of European imperialism also contained an implicit condemnation both of any continued Allied reliance on the old diplomacy of the balance of power and of any Allied failure to live up to liberal values in the future. For the President, then, the League Covenant projected the vision of a liberal world order, transcending the historical and traditional restraints of power politics, into which a liberalized Germany could eventually be reintegrated as a full partner.

Wilson conceived the essence of the League as an orderly social contract among the nations. The international social contract represented by the Covenant of the League was to rescue the world from an insecure "Hobbesian" state of nature in which nations could find temporary security only through armaments and the balance of power. The President saw the League Covenant as establishing a new co-operative international society, governed by liberal norms, whose nation-state members would be pledged to substitute public discussion and peaceful arbitration under world law for the reactionary diplomatic practices of secret diplomacy or armed conflict. Indeed, Wilson always put far more emphasis on the universal moral force of world liberal opinion, focused in an association of self-governing states, than he did on the armed power of the League members.

In Wilson's new "Lockeanized" international environment, in which formerly hostile nations had been theoretically transformed into equal law-abiding liberal world citizens, all countries, weak and strong alike, were to eschew power politics and were also to covenant together, under Article X of the League of Nations Covenant, to defend each other's legal rights and territorial integrity. On one occasion, the President pithily expressed his orderly liberal desire to transform a world political system in which, historically, might had made right, by remarking that he hoped "to make a society instead of a set of barbarians out of the governments of the world." The League Covenant, then, ultimately represented for Wilson the fulfillment of America's historic mission to lead the Old World away from the traditional war-producing diplomacy of the balance of power to an harmonious American-inspired liberal world order of international responsibility under law. In the eyes of the President the League Covenant was the embodiment of American and world liberalism's final triumph over the imperialistic and atavistic restraints of the pre-liberal historical past.

There can be little doubt that, without his faith that the League offered a new liberal beginning in world politics, in which the concept of a universal concert of powers replaced the old notion of a balance of power, the President would not have been willing to involve the United States so permanently in European affairs. Given Wilson's missionary conception of the universality of America's liberal-nationalism, the League legitimized for him the involvement of American power in world politics by permitting him the assumption that, far from being absorbed as another competing element into the traditional global political reality, American strength was enabled, by the League, to enter world politics at the very moment that world politics was transcended by liberal-internationalism. For Wilson America's involvement in world affairs was inseparably joined with America's effort to lead a liberal anti-imperialist transformation of global reality through the League of Nations. In a theoretical sense, then, the League may be seen as Wilson's answer to reintegrationist critics, such as Hoover and Lansing, who feared lest Allied absorption of America's political and economic power might end hopes for the establishment of an American-inspired world of liberal-capitalist harmony.

For Wilson, the ultimate mission of a liberal exceptionalist America was to lead the rest of the world, without socialist revolution, to a universal liberal triumph over all elements of pre-bourgeois reaction and atavistic imperialism. The war years had seen a strengthening of the President's faith that, under his leadership, the United States was fulfilling this historic destiny by uniting America, the Allies, and common peoples of all countries in a liberal people's war on behalf of freedom and the creation of a new anti-imperialist world order. In the postwar period as well, Wilson was more than ever certain that it was the duty of the American state to continue to act selflessly as the leader of world liberalism in the effort to create a new international system free of power politics and Europe's traditional balance of power. In this connection, it is not surprising that the President saw the American-inspired League of Nations as a logical extension, to the entire world, of America's effort, under the Monroe Doctrine, to keep European reaction out of the Western Hemisphere. In essence, therefore, Wilson saw a powerful postwar America as the leader of the liberal opinion of the world, as the selfless and trusted arbiter of international problems, and as the disinterested defender of a new world order against both traditional imperialism and revolutionary socialism. For the President, America's political, economic, and military self-interest was inseparably joined to America's missionary idealism, in the Wilsonian struggle for international liberal stability.

In the final analysis the League of Nations proved to be the central element in the Wilsonian vision of an Americanized postwar world order in which the contradictions of international politics would be resolved in a new liberal harmony. While it is true that the League provided a means to enforce a severe peace on Germany, it is also true that, for Wilson, the League held out the promise of the eventual reintegration of a reformed Germany into an American-inspired liberal-capitalist world order safe from war and/or socialist revolution. Moreover, by maintaining the basic legitimacy of the nation-state system, the League was a logical expression of Wilson's effort, based on his ideology of American liberal-exceptionalism, to combine the leadership of world liberal anti-imperialism with his somewhat contradictory position as the leader of the militarily powerful American nation-state. Finally, by permitting Wilson to link ideologically American nationalism with liberal-internationalism, the League was the culmination of the President's vision of an orderly American-inspired reform of the traditional world political-economy. Such Wilsonian international reform, by using the League to establish a universal liberal-capitalist stability without class conflict, would ultimately defeat both atavistic imperialism and revolutionary socialism, the two mutually reinforcing barriers to the final realization of America's true national interest and pre-eminence in a liberal world order.

Wilson and the Great Debate
Over Collective Security

ARTHUR S. LINK

The greatest single consequence of the War was the changed diplomatic position of the United States following the Armistice. This country, having broken the European stalemate and made defeat of Germany possible, was now the only country with sufficient wealth and power to guarantee the success of the League of Nations and the stability of the postwar order. No one realized this fact better than President Wilson, who therefore made his determined effort to guarantee American ratification of the Versailles Treaty and membership in the League. In the concluding selection, the editor analyzes the impact of Wilson's challenge on the American people and describes the President's last great and unsuccessful battle.

HAVING HELPED TO LAY THE FOUNDATIONS OF A NEW WORLD ORDER in Paris, Wilson returned to the United States in June, 1919, to face the crucial task of winning the approval of the Senate and the support of the people for the Versailles Treaty, the principal part of the Paris settlement.

From Arthur S. Link, *Wilson the Diplomatist: A Look at His Major Foreign Policies*, Baltimore: The Johns Hopkins Press, 1957, pp. 127–156. Reprinted by permission of the Johns Hopkins Press. Most of the footnotes in the original text have been omitted.

During the months following Wilson's homecoming, indeed until the election of 1920, there ensued in the United States a debate no less important than the great debate of 1787 to 1789 over the ratification of the Constitution. At stake in the latter-day discussion was the issue of American participation in a new system of collective security. To a large degree the fate of that experiment and the future peace of the world would depend upon the response that the American people gave.

The facts of the treaty fight are well known, so often and in such detail have historians and biographers told the story of the epic parliamentary struggle between Republicans and Democrats and of the bitter personal controversy between the President and his chief antagonist, Senator Henry Cabot Lodge of Massachusetts. I cannot ignore the forces and factors that cut the channels of the debate and perhaps decisively affected the decisions that the leaders and their followers made. My main purpose in this brief discussion, however, will be to show what has often been obscured by too much concern for dramatic details, namely, the way in which the great debate of 1919–1920 revealed differences in opinion concerning the role that the United States should play in foreign affairs, differences that were fundamental and authentic because they transcended partisanship and personality and have as much relevance for Americans of the mid-twentieth century as they had in Wilson's day.

The lines of battle over ratification of the Treaty of Versailles were first drawn, not after that treaty had been signed, but before Wilson went to Paris, as a consequence of three decisions that he made between October and December of 1918. The first was his decision to issue an appeal to the country on October 25 for the election of a Democratic Congress, and by so doing to make the forthcoming election a specific test of national confidence in his conduct of foreign affairs. The second was his decision to ignore the Senate and the Republican party in discussions of the possible terms of the settlement and in the appointment of the American delegation to the Paris conference, and to name only such men as he thought would be loyal to him and his ideals and subordinate to his direction. The third was Wilson's decision to go to Paris in person, as the head of the American commission.

The first two decisions were certainly egregious mistakes. On the other hand, Wilson was probably right in deciding that he had to go to Paris to take personal leadership in the fight for a liberal peace. However, the important point is not whether Wilson acted wisely or foolishly; it is the way in which his preparations for the peace conference predetermined the shape of the battle over the treaty that would be signed. By appealing for the election of a Democratic Congress on the ground that a Republican victory would imply a repudiation of his leadership in foreign affairs, and by appointing a peace commission composed with one unimportant exception of Democrats, Wilson made a partisan division on the issues of peace inevitable. In other words, he made it certain that Republicans would oppose and Democrats would support whatever treaty he might help to write. Moreover, by first ignoring the Senate in his appointment of the commissioners, and then by going himself to Paris, Wilson made it inevitable that the treaty fight would renew in virulent form the old conflict between the President and the upper house for control of foreign policy.

While Wilson was in Paris there were unmistakable signs at home that he would encounter bitter opposition when he returned with his peace treaty. The most ominous of these was the so-called "Round Robin" resolution that Senator Lodge presented to the upper house on March 4, 1919. Signed by thirty-seven senators, it declared that the Covenant of the League of Nations, "in the form now proposed to the peace conference," was unacceptable. At the same time, frankly isolationist opponents of the League were beginning a furious rhetorical attack in the Senate chamber.

Although there were limits beyond which Wilson would not go in compromise, as he said in a New York address on the eve of his return to France after a brief visit to the United States in late February and early March of 1919, he yielded to the advice of friends who urged him to conciliate his critics. For example, he endeavored to assuage the signers of the "Round Robin" resolution by permitting Henry White, the Republican member of the American peace delegation, to attempt to ascertain from Lodge why the Covenant was unacceptable to them. Or again, after Lodge had refused to answer specifically, Wilson took the advice of former President William Howard Taft and other Republican supporters of the League and obtained amendments to meet certain American criticisms of the Covenant.[1]

Undertaken reluctantly at best, these measures did little to conciliate the extreme opposition or to conceal Wilson's true feelings about his senatorial critics and his growing determination to defy them. The more he had to concede at Paris during the final months of the conference, the more this determination hardened. By the time he signed the Versailles Treaty, Wilson was obviously sick of making compromises and eager to return to a political arena in which he could fight hard again, without the necessity of giving ground to opponents who had as much power as he. "I have found one can never get anything in this life that is worth while without fighting

---

[1] These amendments provided for the right of members of the League to withdraw after giving due notice, exempted domestic questions from the jurisdiction of the League, permitted member nations to refuse to accept a colonial mandate, and accorded formal recognition to the Monroe Doctrine.

for it," he told Colonel House, who had urged him to meet the Senate in a conciliatory spirit, on the day that he left Paris.

•   •   •

Wilson was, therefore, in the mood of a triumphant leader presenting his adversaries with a *fait accompli* when he presented the treaty formally to the Senate on July 10. He did not refer to the senators, as he had often done before, as his "colleagues" in the conduct of foreign relations, nor did he use his favorite phrase "common counsel" or talk about the necessity of agreement among reasonable men. On the contrary, after "informing" the senators that a world settlement had been made, he took the highest possible ground to urge prompt and unqualified approval of the treaty. The League of Nations, he exclaimed, was the hope of mankind. "Dare we reject it and break the heart of the world?" He reiterated the answer in an impromptu peroration at the end:

The stage is set, the destiny disclosed. It has come about by no plan of our conceiving, but by the hand of God who led us into this way. We cannot turn back. We can only go forward, with lifted eyes and freshened spirit, to follow the vision. It was of this that we dreamed at our birth. America shall in truth show the way. The light streams upon the path ahead, and nowhere else.

Many historians have been frankly puzzled by Wilson's refusal even to attempt to build support for the peace settlement in the Senate and the Republican party—among the very men who would have the power of life or death over the Treaty of Versailles. How could an authority on the American constitutional system have forgotten the Senate's jealous role in foreign affairs? How could an intelligent and astute political strategist have done the things best calculated to assure the defeat of plans upon which he thought depended the future happiness of mankind? The dilemma inherent in these hyperbolic questions is much more apparent than real. In fact, it is not too much to say that Wilson acted in the only way that it was possible for him to act, given his convictions concerning the President's control over foreign relations, his belief in party responsibility, his view of public opinion, and his own temperament.

. . . Wilson believed that the President was a virtual sovereign, responsible only to public opinion and not to Congress, in the conduct of external affairs. In ignoring the Senate in the appointment of the peace commission, in taking personal responsibility for writing the peace treaty, and in standing defiantly in its defense, he was, therefore, simply playing the constitutional role that he thought was proper for the chief executive. Given Wilson's views of party responsibility, moreover, it was inevitable that he should have ignored the Republican opposition in the processes of peace-making, because he could not work in harmony with men whose duty he knew it would be to oppose him at every turn. Given Wilson's urge to dominate and his belief that the Republican leaders, particularly Senator Lodge, represented all the dark forces against which he was battling, it is difficult to imagine him sharing responsibility or dealing with his opponents on a give-and-take basis after his return from Paris.

These are reasons enough to explain the President's methods and his posture of defiance at the beginning of the treaty fight. There was another reason that was more important than all the rest—Wilson's supreme confidence in his own creation and in the overwhelming support of the American people. He knew not only that he was right, but that the people would know that he was right and would crush any man who dared to obstruct the fulfillment of the age-old dream of peace. That was what he meant when he told reporters that of course the Senate would ratify the Versailles Treaty. . . .

Actually, the situation was far less simple and reassuring than Wilson imagined at the beginning of the great debate. For one thing, powerful voices were already raised in outright and violent condemnation of the treaty on various grounds. There were the idealists who had thrilled at Wilson's vision of a new world and who now drew back in disgust because the treaty failed to establish a millennial order. There were the so-called hyphenate groups—the German-Americans, who believed that the treaty was a base betrayal of the Fatherland; the Italian-Americans, who were sulking over Wilson's opposition to Italy's demands; and, most important, the several million Irish-Americans, inflamed by the civil war then raging in Ireland, who were up in arms because Wilson had refused to press the cause of Irish independence at Paris and because the treaty allegedly benefited the hated English. There was the powerful chain of Hearst newspapers, marshaling and inciting all the hyphenate protests. There were the out-and-out isolationists, who believed that American membership in the League of Nations would mean entanglement in all of Europe's rivalries and wars. They had powerful advocates in a small group of so-called irreconcilables or bitter-enders in the Senate, led by Hiram Johnson of California, William E. Borah of Idaho, and James A. Reed of Missouri, who opposed the treaty for nationalistic reasons of their own divination.

These were the major groups who opposed ratification of the treaty. In the ensuing debate they were perhaps the loudest and busiest participants of all. They were, however, a minority among the leaders of thought and political opinion, and they spoke for a minority of the people, at least before 1920 if not afterward. This is a simple point but a vital one, because in its important aspects the debate over the treaty was not a struggle between advocates of complete withdrawal on the one side and proponents of total international commitment on the other. It was, rather, a contest between the champions of a strong system of collective security and a group who favored a more limited commitment in international affairs. It was a choice between these alternatives, and not between complete isolation or complete internationalism, that the President, the Senate, and the American people eventually had to make. For this reason, therefore, I propose to let the arguments of the isolationists pass without analyzing them, and to concentrate my attention upon the two main and decisive courses of the debate.

Before we do this, it might be well to remind ourselves of the precise issues at stake. There were differences of opinion in the United States over the territorial and other provisions of the treaty, to be sure, but all of them were insignificant as compared to the differences evoked by the Covenant of the League and its provisions for universal collective security. Those provisions were clear and for the most part unequivocal. There was, of course, Article 10, which guaranteed the political independence and territorial integrity of every member nation throughout the world. There were, besides, Articles 11, 12, 13, 15, 16, and 17, which established the machinery of arbitration for all international disputes susceptible to that procedure and decreed that an act of war against one member nation should "*ipso facto* be deemed to . . . [be] an act of war against all the other Members" and should be followed automatically by an economic blockade against the aggressor and by Council action to determine what military measures should be used to repel the aggression. These were almost ironclad guarantees of mutual security, meant to be effective and unencumbered by the right of any nation involved in a dispute to veto action by the League's Council. Whether such a world-wide system could work, and whether the American people were prepared at this stage of their development to support such a system even if it did—these were the two main issues of the great debate of 1919–1920.

The decisive opposition to the Versailles Treaty came from a group of men who to a varying degree gave negative answers to both these questions. This group included some of the most distinguished leaders in the Senate and out, men like Senator Frank B. Kellogg of Minnesota, Nicholas Murray Butler, former Secretary of State Elihu Root, Charles Evans Hughes, and Herbert Hoover. Most of them were Republicans, because few Democrats active in politics dared to incur the President's wrath by opposing him. They were not isolationists, but limited internationalists who in a varying degree believed that the United States should play an active role in preserving the peace of the world. Most of them favored, for example, arbitration, the establishment of something like a World Court to interpret and codify international law, and international agreements for disarmament, economic co-operation, and the like. Some of them even supported the idea of alliances with certain powers for specific purposes.

On the other hand, all the limited internationalists opposed any such approval of the treaty as would commit the United States unreservedly to such a system of collective security as the Covenant of the League had created. Their arguments might be summarized as follows:

First, a system of collective security that is world-wide in operation is not likely either to work or to endure the strains that will inevitably be put upon it, because in practice the great powers will not accept the limitations that the Covenant places upon their sovereignty, and no nation will go to war to vindicate Article 10 unless its vital interests compel it to do so. Such sweeping guarantees as the Covenant affords are, therefore, worse than no guarantees at all because they offer only an illusory hope of security.

Second, the Covenant's fundamental guarantee, embodied in Article 10, is impossible to maintain because its promise to perpetuate the *status quo* defies the very law of life. As Elihu Root put it:

If perpetual, it would be an attempt to preserve for all time unchanged the distribution of power and territory made in accordance with the views and exigencies of the Allies in this present juncture of affairs. It would necessarily be futile. . . . It would not only be futile; it would be mischievous. Change and growth are the law of life, and no generation can impose its will in regard to the growth of nations and the distribution of power, upon succeeding generations.

Third, the American people are not ready to support the Covenant's sweeping commitments and in fact should not do so unless their vital interests are involved in a dispute. They would and should be ready to act to prevent the outbreak of any conflict that threatened to lead to a general war, but it is inconceivable that they would or should assume the risk of war to prevent a border dispute in the Balkans, or to help maintain Japanese control of the Shantung Province or British supremacy in Ireland and India. Unconditional ratification of the treaty by the United States would, therefore, be worse than outright rejection, for it would mean the making of promises that the American people could not possibly honor in the future.

Fourth, unqualified membership in the League will raise grave dangers to American interests and the American constitutional system. It will menace American control over immigration and tariff policies, imperil the

Monroe Doctrine, increase the power of the President at the expense of Congress, and necessitate the maintenance of a large standing army for the fulfillment of obligations under the Covenant.

Fifth, and most important, full-fledged participation in such a system of collective security as the Covenant establishes will spell the end of American security in foreign affairs, because it will mean transferring the power of decision over questions of peace and war from the President and Congress to an international agency which the United States could not control.

Voicing these objections day in and out as the great debate reached its crescendo in the autumn of 1919, the limited internationalists made their purposes and program indelibly clear. They would accept most of the provisions of the treaty unrelated to the League and acquiesce in the ones that they did not like. They would also sanction American membership in the League of Nations. But they would also insist upon reserving to the United States, and specifically to Congress, the power of decision concerning the degree of American participation in the League; and they would make no binding promise to enforce collective security anywhere in the future.

This was also the position of Senator Lodge, the man who devised and executed the Republican strategy in the upper house during the parliamentary phase of the treaty struggle. Personally, Lodge had little hope for the success of the League, a profound personal contempt for Wilson, and almost a sardonic scorn for the President's international ideals. The Massachusetts senator was an ardent nationalist, almost a jingoist, no isolationist, but a believer in a strong balance of power. His solution would have been harsh terms, including dismemberment, for Germany and the formation of an Anglo-Franco-American alliance as the best insurance for future peace. But as chairman of the Foreign Relations Committee and leader of his party in the Senate, it was his duty to sublimate his own strong feelings and to find a common ground upon which most Republicans could stand. That common ground, that program acceptable to an overwhelming majority of Republicans inside the Senate and out, was, in brief, to approve the treaty and accept membership in the League, subject to certain amendments and reservations that would achieve the objectives of the limited internationalists.

Debated all through the late summer of 1919, these amendments and reservations were embodied in the report that the Republican majority of the Foreign Relations Committee presented to the upper house on September 10. During the following weeks the Senate rejected the amendments and adopted most of them in the form of reservations, fourteen in all.

Most of them were unimportant, but there was one that constituted a virtual rejection of the system of collective security that Wilson had constructed. It was Reservation 2, which declared that the United States assumed no obligations to preserve the territorial integrity or political independence of any other country, unless Congress should by act or joint resolution specifically assume such an obligation. In addition, the preamble to the reservations provided that American ratification of the treaty should not take effect until at least three of the four principal Allied powers had accepted the reservations in a formal exchange of notes.

This, then, was the program to which most of Wilson's opponents stood committed by the time that the Senate moved toward a formal vote on the Versailles Treaty. Whether Lodge himself was an irreconcilable who desired the defeat of the treaty, or whether he was merely a strong reservationist is an important question, but an irrelevant one at this point. The significant fact is that he had succeeded in uniting most Republicans and in commiting them to a program that affirmed limited internationalism at the same time that it repudiated American support of collective security for virtually the entire world.

Meanwhile, despite his earlier show of intransigence, Wilson had been hard at work in preparation for the impending struggle. In an effort to split the Republican ranks, he held a series of conferences in late July with eleven moderate Republican senators who were called mild reservationists because they favored approval of the treaty after the adoption of a few interpretive reservations. On August 19 the President met the Foreign Relations Committee at the White House for a three-hour grilling on all phases of the settlement. In spite of these overtures, there were unmistakable signs that Wilson had failed to win the support of any large number of Republican senators and that the strong reservationists and isolationists were rapidly gaining ground in the debate that was now proceeding in full fury throughout the country.

In response, Wilson made one of the most fateful decisions of his career. It was, as he put it, to go to the people and purify the wells of public opinion that had been poisoned by the isolationists and opponents of unreserved ratification. He was physically weakened by his labors at Paris, and his physician warned that a long speaking tour might endanger his life. Even so, he insisted upon making the effort to rally the people, the sources of authority, who had always sustained him in the past.

Leaving Washington on September 3, 1919, Wilson headed for the heartland of America, into Ohio, Indiana, Missouri, Iowa, Nebraska, Minnesota, and the Dakotas—into the region where isolationist sentiment was strongest. From there he campaigned through the Northwest and the major cities of the Pacific Coast. The final leg of his journey took him through Nevada, Utah, Wyoming, and Colorado, where the tour ended after Wilson's partial breakdown on September 25 and 26. In all he traveled 8,000 miles in twenty-two days and delivered thirty-two major addresses and eight minor ones. It was not only the greatest speaking effort of Wilson's career, but also one of the most notable forensic accomplishments in American history.

Everywhere that he went Wilson pleaded in good temper, not as a partisan, but as a leader who stood above party strife and advantage. He made his tour, he explained, first of all so that the people might know the truth about the Treaty of Versailles and no longer be confused by the misrepresentations of its enemies. As he put it at Oakland and at Reno:

One thing has been impressed upon me more than another as I have crossed the continent, and that is that the people of the United States have been singularly and, I some times fear deliberately, misled as to the character and contents of the treaty of peace.

Some of the critics . . . are looking backward. . . . Their power to divert, or to pervert, the view of this whole thing has made it necessary for me repeatedly on this journey to take the liberty that I am going to take with you to-night, of telling you just what kind of a treaty this is.

In almost every speech, therefore, Wilson explicitly described and defended the major provisions of the treaty and the purposes of its framers. He defended the severity of the articles relating to Germany, on the ground that her crimes against civilization demanded stern punishment. He answered the critics of the Shantung settlement, first by frankly admitting that he did not like the provisions for Japanese control and next by declaring that he had obtained the only possible settlement that offered any hope for China's eventual recovery of the province. In a similar manner he tried to answer other criticisms, and he concluded, not by denying that there were imperfections in the treaty, but by declaring that they were more than counterbalanced by the constructive achievements.

Wilson's supreme purpose was, of course, not to explain the controverted provisions of the treaty relating to territories, colonies, and reparations, but rather to defend the League of Nations against its traducers, to explain the system of collective security that its Covenant had established, and to call the American people to the world leadership that he said history now demanded of them.

He began usually by telling how the League of Nations was the fulfillment of an old American dream of peace, how it was an attempt to apply the principles of the Monroe Doctrine to the world at large, how the suggestion of such an organization had come in recent times as much if not more from Republicans than from Democrats, and how he had simply translated American ideas and proposals into statutory form and insisted that they be embodied in the treaty.

The President then proceeded to describe the provisions of the Covenant for collective security, to show how they would work in actual practice, and to attempt to prove that they afforded a system for peace instead of for war. Article 10, he was fond of emphasizing, was the heart of the Covenant and the foundation of the new world order. "Article X," he said at Indianapolis, "speaks the conscience of the world." "Article X," he added at Reno,

is the heart of the enterprise. Article X is the test of the honor and courage and endurance of the world. Article X says that every member of the League, and that means every great fighting power in the world, . . . solemnly engages to respect and preserve as against external aggression the territorial integrity and existing political independence of the other members of the League. If you do that, you have absolutely stopped ambitious and aggressive war . . . , [for] as against external aggression, as against ambition, as against the desire to dominate from without, we all stand together in a common pledge, and that pledge is essential to the peace of the world.

In answer to critics who had argued that unconditional affirmation of Article 10 would involve the United States perpetually in war, Wilson replied by attempting to demonstrate that future wars would be virtually impossible and almost unnecessary if the collective security provisions of the Covenant implementing Article 10 was observed and enforced by the members of the League. To begin with, nations engaged in a dispute that might lead to war were bound to submit their controversy either to arbitration, the World Court, or the Council of the League. Should any nation go to war in violation of these promises, then all the other members of the League would automatically institute a total blockade, "financial, commercial, and personal," against the aggressor.

As Wilson explained at Kansas City:

We absolutely boycott them [the aggressors]. . . . There shall be no communication even between them and the rest of the world. They shall receive no goods; they shall ship no goods. They shall receive no telegraphic messages; they shall send none. They shall receive no mail; no mail will be received from them. The nationals, the citizens, of the member states will never enter their territory until the matter is adjusted, and their citizens cannot leave their territory. It is the most complete boycott ever conceived in a public document, and I want to say to you with confident prediction that there will be no more fighting after that.

It was possible, of course, Wilson admitted, that war would occur in spite of all these precautions. "Nobody in his senses claims for the Covenant . . . that it is certain to stop war," he said at Indianapolis. If an aggressor flaunted the provisions of the Covenant, and if economic measures did not suffice to stop the aggression, then war would probably occur. If it were a major conflagration, then the United States could not remain neutral in any event. If it were a minor controversy far removed from the Western Hemisphere, then the United States would not be directly involved. Enemies of the League had charged that membership in that body would mean American involvement in every dispute everywhere in the world. "If you want to put out a fire in Utah," the President replied at Salt Lake City,

you do not send to Oklahoma for the fire engine. If you want to put out a fire in the Balkans, if you want to stamp out the smoldering flame in some part of central Europe, you do not send to the United States for troops. The Council of the League selects the powers which are most ready, most available, most suitable, and selects them only at their own consent, so that the United States would in no such circumstances conceivably be drawn in unless the flame spread to the world.

To the charge that membership in the League would impair American sovereignty and require the fulfillment of unpleasant duties, Wilson replied that the contention was, of course, true in part. "The only way in which you can have impartial determinations to this world is by consenting to something you do not want to do," he said at Billings, Montana.

Every time you have a case in court one or the other of the parties has to consent to do something he does not want to do. . . . Yet we regard that as the foundation of civilization, that we will not fight about these things, and that when we lose in court we will take our medicine.

It seemed almost superfluous, Wilson added, to argue the necessity of American membership in the League of Nations. There was the obvious fact, he declared at Des Moines, that American isolation had ended,

not because we chose to go into the politics of the world, but because by the sheer genius of this people and the growth of our power we have become a determining factor in the history of mankind, and after you have become a determining factor you cannot remain isolated, whether you want to or not.

The only question confronting the American people was, therefore, whether they would exercise their influence in the world, which could henceforth be profound and controlling, in partnership with the other powers or in defiance of them. Standing alone, he warned, meant defying the world; defying the world meant maintaining a great standing army and navy; and such militarism and navalism meant the end of democracy at home.

There was the additional fact that without American participation and leadership the League of Nations would become merely another armed alliance instead of a true concert of power. "It would be an alliance," Wilson declared at St. Louis,

in which the partnership would be between the more powerful European nations and Japan, and the . . . antagonist, the disassociated party, the party standing off to be watched by the alliance, would be the United States of America. There can be no league of nations in the true sense without the partnership of this great people.

Without American participation and leadership, therefore, the League would fail. Without the League there could be no effective collective security system. Without collective security, wars would come again. American participation was, therefore, essential to peace, the most vital and elemental interest of the United States. This became increasingly the main theme of Wilson's addresses as he journeyed deeper into the West. Over and over he cried out warnings like these:

Ah, my fellow citizens, do not forget the aching hearts that are behind discussions like this. Do not forget the forlorn homes from which those boys went and to which they never came back. I have it in my heart that if we do not do this great thing now, every woman ought to weep because of the child in her arms. If she has a boy at her breast, she may be sure that when he comes to manhood this terrible task will have to be done once more. Everywhere we go, the train when it stops is surrounded with little children, and I look at them almost with tears in my eyes, because I feel my mission is to save them. These glad youngsters with flags in their hands—I pray God that they may never have to carry that flag upon the battlefield!

Why, my fellow citizens, nothing brings a lump into my throat quicker on this journey I am taking than to see the thronging children that are everywhere the first, just out of childish curiosity and glee, no doubt, to crowd up to the train when it stops, because I know that if by any chance we should not win this great fight for the League of Nations it would be their death warrant. They belong to the generation which would then have to fight the final war, and in that final war there would not be merely seven and a half million men slain. The very existence of civilization would be in the balance. . . . Stop for a moment to think about the next war, if there should be one. I do not hesitate to say that the war we have just been through, though it was shot through with terror of every kind, is not to be compared with the war we would have to face next time. . . . Ask any soldier if he wants to go through a hell like that again. The soldiers know what the next war would be. They know what the inventions were that were just about to be used for the absolute destruction of mankind. I am for any kind of insurance against a barbaric reversal of civilization.

Who were the enemies of the League and of the future peace of the world? They were, Wilson declared, the outright isolationists and the men who would destroy the charter of mankind by crippling reservations. They were little Americans, provincials, men of narrow vision. "They are ready to go back to that old and ugly plan of armed nations, of alliances, of watchful jealousies, of rabid antagonisms, of purposes concealed, running by the subtle channels of intrigue through the veins of people who do not dream what poison is being injected into their systems." "When at last in the annals of mankind they are gibbeted, they will regret that the gibbet is so high."

One by one Wilson answered the specific criticisms of the Covenant relating to the Monroe Doctrine, the right of members to withdraw, and the question whether the League had any jurisdiction over the domestic affairs of member nations. He told how he had obtained revision of the Covenant to satisfy American doubts about its first draft. These amendments, he continued, were embodied in the Covenant and were written in language as explicit as he knew how to devise. He would not object to reservations that merely clarified the American understanding of these questions. Reservations that in any way changed the meaning of the Covenant were, however, more serious, because they would require the renegotiation of the treaty.

There remained the greatest threat of all to the integrity of the Covenant, the challenge of the Lodge reservations to Article 10. This reservation, Wilson warned, would destroy the foundations of collective security, because it was a notice to the world that the American people would fulfill their obligations only when it suited their purposes to do so. "That," the President exclaimed at Salt Lake City, "is a rejection of the Covenant. That is an absolute refusal to carry any part of the same responsibility that the other members of the League carry." "In other words, my fellow citizens," he added at Cheyenne,

what this proposes is this: That we should make no general promise, but leave the nations associated with us to guess in each instance what we were going to consider ourselves bound to do and what we were not going to consider ourselves bound to do. It is as if you said, "We will not join the League definitely, but we will join it occasionally. We will not promise anything, but from time to time we may coöperate. We will not assume any obligations." . . . This reservation proposes that we should not acknowledge any moral obligation in the matter; that we should stand off and say, "We will see, from time to time; consult us when you get into trouble, and then we will have a debate, and after two or three months we will tell you what we are going to do." The thing is unworthy and ridiculous, and I want to say distinctly that, as I read this, it would change the entire meaning of the treaty and exempt the United States from all responsibility for the preservation of peace. It means the rejection of the treaty, my fellow countrymen, nothing less. It means that the United States would take from under the structure its very foundations and support.

The irony of it all was, Wilson added, that the reservation was actually unnecessary, *if the objective of its framers was merely to reserve the final decision for war to the American government.* In the case of all disputes to which it was not a party, the United States would have an actual veto over the Council's decision for war, because that body could not advise member nations to go to war except by unanimous vote, exclusive of the parties to the dispute. Thus, the President explained, there was absolutely no chance that the United States could be forced into war against its will, unless it was itself guilty of aggression, in which case it would be at war anyway.

These were, Wilson admitted, legal technicalities, and, he added, he would not base his case for American participation in the League of Nations upon them. The issue was not who had the power to make discisions for war, but whether the American people were prepared to go whole-heartedly into the League, determined to support its collective system un-reservedly, and willing to make the sacrifices that were necessary to preserve peace. Wilson summarized all his pleading with unrivaled feeling at the Mormon capital, as follows:

Instead of wishing to ask to stand aside, get the benefits of the League, but share none of its burdens or responsibilities, I for my part want to go in and accept what is offered to us, the leadership of the world. A leadership of what sort, my fellow citizens? Not a leadership that leads men along the lines by which great nations can profit out of weak nations, not an exploiting power, but a liberating power, a power to show the world that when America was born it was indeed a finger pointed toward those lands into which men could deploy some of these days and live in happy freedom, look each other in the eyes as equals, see that no man was put upon, that no people were forced to accept authority which was not of their own choice, and that out of the general generous impulse of the human genius and the human spirit we were gifted along the levels of civilization to days when there should be wars no more, but men should govern themselves in peace and amity and quiet. That is the leadership we said we wanted, and now the world offers it to us. It is inconceivable that we should reject it.

We come now to the well-known tragic sequel. Following his address at Pueblo, Colorado, on September 25, 1919, the President showed such obvious signs of exhaustion that his physician canceled his remaining en-gagements and sped the Presidential train to Washington. On October 2

Wilson suffered a severe stroke and paralysis of the left side of his face and body. For several days his life hung in the balance; then he gradually revived, and by the end of October he was clearly out of danger. But his recovery was only partial at best. His mind remained relatively clear; but he was physically enfeebled, and the disease had wrecked his emotional constitution and aggravated all his more unfortunate personal traits.

Meanwhile, the Senate was nearing the end of its long debate over the Treaty of Versailles. Senator Lodge presented his revised fourteen reservations on behalf of the Foreign Relations Committee to the upper house on November 6, 1919. Senator Gilbert M. Hitchcock of Nebraska, the Democratic minority leader, countered with five reservations, four of which Wilson had approved in substance before he embarked upon his western tour. They simply sought to make clear the American understanding of Article 10 and other provisions of the treaty. The issue before the Senate was, therefore, now clear—whether to approve the treaty with reservations that did not impair the American obligation to enforce collective security, or whether to approve the treaty with reservations that repudiated all compelling obligations and promised American support for only a limited international system.

Lodge beat down the Hitchcock reservations with the help of the irreconcilables and then won adoption of his own. Now the President had to choose between ratification with the Lodge reservations or running the risk of the outright defeat of the treaty. He gave his decision to Hitchcock in a brief conference at the White House on November 17 and in a letter on the following day: Under no circumstances could he accept the Lodge reservation to Article 10, for it meant nullification of the treaty. When the Senate voted on November 19, therefore, most of the Democrats joined the irreconcilable to defeat ratification with the Lodge reservations by a count of thirty-nine ayes to fifty-five nays. Hoping to split the Republican ranks and win the support of the "mild reservationists," the Democratic leaders then moved unconditional approval of the treaty. This strategy, upon which Wilson had placed all his hopes, failed, as a firm Republican majority defeated the resolution with the help of the irreconcilables by a vote of thirty-eight ayes to fifty-three nays.

It was not the end, for during the following months an overwhelming majority of the leaders of opinion in the United States refused to accept the Senate's vote as the final verdict. In the absence of any reliable indices, it is impossible to measure the division of public opinion as a whole; but there can be little doubt that an overwhelming majority of thoughtful people favored ratification with some kind of reservations, and even with the Lodge reservations, if that were necessary to obtain the Senate's consent.

There was, consequently, enormous pressure upon the leaders in both parties for compromise during the last weeks of 1919 and the early months of 1920. Prominent Republicans who had taken leadership in a nonpartisan campaign for the League, including former President Taft and President A. Lawrence Lowell of Harvard University; scores of editors and the spokesmen of various academic, religious, and labor organizations; and Democratic leaders who dared oppose the President, like William J. Bryan and Colonel House, begged Lodge and Wilson to find a common ground. Alarmed by the possibility of American rejection of the treaty, spokesmen for the British government declared publicly that limited American participation in the League would be better than no participation at all.

Under this pressure the moderate leaders in both camps set to work in late December and early January to find a basis for agreement. Even Lodge began to weaken and joined the bipartisan conferees who were attempting to work out an acceptable reservation to Article 10. But the Massachusetts senator and his friend would not yield the essence of their reservation, and it was Wilson who had to make the final choice. By January he had recovered sufficient physical strength to manage his forces in the upper house. All the while, however, his intransigence had been compounded by personal bitterness and by the growing conviction that rejection of the treaty was preferable to a dishonorable ratification. Consequently, between January and March, 1920, when the final debates and maneuvers were in progress, he rejected all suggestions of yielding on Article 10. Instead, he apparently began to make fantastic plans to run again for the presidency in a campaign that would decide the fate of the treaty. "If there is any doubt as to what the people of the country think on this vital matter," he wrote in a letter to the Democratic party on January 8, 1920, "the clear and single way out is to submit it for determination at the next election to the voters of the Nation, to give the next election the form of a great and solemn referendum."

Thus the parliamentary phase of the struggle moved to its inexorable conclusion when the Senate took its second and final vote on the treaty on March 19, 1920. The only hope for approval lay in the chance that enough Democrats would defy the President, as many friends of the League were urging them to do, to obtain a two-thirds majority for ratification with the Lodge reservations. Twenty-one Democrats did follow their consciences rather than the command from the White House, but not enough of them defected to put the treaty across. The treaty with the Lodge reservations failed by seven votes.

There was a final sequel. The Democratic Presidential and Vice-Presidential candidates, James M. Cox and Franklin D. Roosevelt, tried hard to make the election of 1920 a "great and solemn referendum" on the League. But the effort failed, because so many other issues were involved, because the Republican candidate, Warren G. Harding, equivocated so artfully that no one knew where he stood, and because virtually all the distinguished leaders of the G.O.P. assured the country that a Republican victory promised the best hope of American membership in the League. These promises were obviously not honored. One of the new President's first official acts was to repudiate the idea of membership in the League; one of the new administration's first foreign policies was to conclude a separate peace with Germany.

Virtually all historians now agree that Wilson's refusal to permit his followers in the Senate to approve the treaty with the Lodge reservations was an error of tragic magnitude. Having built so grandly at Paris, having fought so magnificently at home for his creation, he then proceeded by his own hand to remove the cornerstone of his edifice of peace. Why? Were there inner demons of pride and arrogance driving him to what one historian has called "the supreme infanticide"? Did his illness and seclusion prevent him from obtaining a realistic view of the parliamentary situation, or so disarrange him emotionally that he became incompetent in the tasks of statesmanship?[1] Or was he simply an idealist who would make no compromises on what he thought were fundamental principles?

The historian, who sees through a glass darkly when probing the recesses of the mind, is not able to give final answers to questions like these. Wilson, for all his high-mindedness and nobility of character, was headstrong and not much given to dealing graciously or to compromising with men whom he distrusted and disliked. Once before, in a violent dispute at Princeton over control of the graduate school, he had revealed these same traits and suffered defeat because he could not work with men whom he did not trust. The sympathetic biographer would like to believe that it was his illness, which aggravated his bitterness and his sense of self-righteousness, that drove Wilson to his fatal choice. Perhaps this is true. He had not always been incapable of compromise; perhaps he would have yielded in the end if disease had not dethroned his reason.

These attempts to extenuate ignore the fact that there were fundamental and vital issues at stake in the controversy over the treaty—whether the United States would take leadership in the League of Nations without hesitations and reservations, or whether it would join the League grudgingly and with no promises to help maintain universal collective security.

---

[1] Edwin A. Weinstein, M.D., "Denial of Presidential Disability: A Case Study of Woodrow Wilson," *Psychiatry* (Washington), XXX (Nov. 1967), 376–391. Dr. Weinstein argues persuasively that this was in fact the case. [*Editor's note.*]

To Wilson the difference between what he fought for and what Lodge and the Republicans would agree to was the difference between the success or failure and the life or death of man's best hope for peace. This he had said on his western tour, at a time when his health and reasoning faculties were unimpaired. This he believed with his heart and soul. It is, therefore, possible, even probable, that Wilson would have acted as he did even had he not suffered his breakdown, for it was not in his nature to compromise away the principles in which he believed.

If this is true, then in this, the last and greatest effort of his life, Wilson spurned the role of statesman for what he must have thought was the nobler role of prophet. The truth is that the American people were not prepared in 1920 to assume the world leadership that Wilson offered them, and that the powers of the world were not yet ready to enforce the world-wide, universal system of collective security that the President had created.

Collective security failed in the portentous tests of the 1930's, not because the League's machinery was defective, but because the people of the world, not merely the American people alone, were unwilling to confront aggressors with the threat of war. As a result a second and more terrible world conflict came, as Wilson prophesied it would, and at its end the United States helped to build a new and different league of nations and took the kind of international leadership that Wilson had called for. But events of the past decade have not fully justified Wilson's confidence in international organization; the only really promising systems of collective security, the regional ones like NATO, have been of a kind that Wilson fervently denounced; and only the future can reveal whether his dream of a universal system can ever be made a reality.

And so it was Wilson the prophet, demanding greater commitment, sacrifice, and idealism than the people could give, who was defeated in 1920. It is also Wilson the prophet who survives in history, in the hopes and aspirations of mankind and in whatever ideals of international service that the American people still cherish. One thing is certain, now that men have the power to sear virtually the entire face of the earth: The prophet of 1919 was right in his larger vision; the challenge that he raised then is today no less real and no less urgent than it was in his own time.

SELECTIVE BIBLIOGRAPHY

For general surveys of the entire period, 1914–1920, with special emphasis on Wilson, see Harley Notter, *The Origins of the Foreign Policy of Woodrow Wilson* (1939); Arthur S. Link, *Wilson the Diplomatist: A Look at His Major Foreign Policies* (1957); N. Gordon Levin, Jr., *Woodrow Wilson and World Politics: America's Response to War and Revolution* (1968); Charles Seymour, *American Diplomacy during the World War* (1934); and Arthur S. Link and William B. Catton, *American Epoch: A History of the United States Since the 1890's* (1967).

The impact of the World War upon American public opinion is most fully covered by Arthur S. Link, *Wilson: The Struggle for Neutrality* (1960); *Wilson: Confusions and Crises* (1964); *Wilson: Campaigns for Progressivism and Peace* (1965); and—in an abridgement of these three volumes—*Woodrow Wilson and the Progressive Era* (1954). Robert E. Osgood, *Ideals and Self-Interest in America's Foreign Relations* (1953); has a provocative chapter on the First World War. Horace C. Peterson, *Propaganda for War* (1939), and George S. Viereck, *Spreading Germs of Hate* (1930), cover the impact of British and German propaganda even though both books overrate the significance of that propaganda.

For Wilson's responses to challenges during the period of American neutrality, 1914–1917, the most detailed coverage is to be found in Link's *Wilson: Struggle for Neutrality, Wilson: Confusions and Crises,* and *Wilson: Campaigns for Progressivism and Peace,* just cited. Briefer and provocative versions of the same story are Ernest R. May, *The World War and American Isolation* (1959); Edward H. Buehrig, *Woodrow Wilson and the Balance of Power* (1955); and Charles Seymour, *American Neutrality, 1914–1917* (1935).

The literature on wartime diplomacy, particularly about the impact of Wilsonian diplomacy during this period, is burgeoning at a prodigious rate, and only the most notable works on the subject can be mentioned: Arno J. Mayer, *Political Origins of the New Diplomacy* (1959); Victor S. Mamatey, *The United States and East Central Europe, 1914–1918* (1957); George F. Kennan, *Russia Leaves the War* (1956) and *The Decision to Intervene* (1958); and Laurence W. Martin, *Peace Without Victory: Woodrow Wilson and the British Liberals* (1958).

Seward W. Livermore, *Politics Is Adjourned: Woodrow Wilson and the War Congress, 1916–1918* (1966) is the best work thus far on domestic politics during wartime. We still have no good single study of the American war mobilization, but the reader may piece the story together from William E. Leuchtenburg, "The New Deal and the Analogue of War," in John Braeman *et al.* (eds.), *Change and Continuity in Twentieth-Century America* (1964); Allen F. Davis, "Welfare, Reform and World War I," *American Quarterly*, XIX (Fall of 1967), 516–533; Daniel R. Beaver, *Newton D. Baker and the American War Effort, 1917–1919* (1966); Bernard M. Baruch, *American Industry in War* (1941); and specialized studies like Alexander D. Noyes, *The War Period of American Finance, 1908–1925* (1926), and Sidney Ratner, *Taxation and Democracy in America* (1967).

For the government's propaganda campaign and the various drives to silence dissenters, the following are excellent: James R. Mock and Cedric Larson, *Words that Won the War* (1939); Horace C. Peterson and Gilbert C. Fite, *Opponents of War, 1917–1918* (1957); Donald D. Johnson, *The Challenge to American Freedoms: World War I and the Rise of the American Civil Liberties Union* (1963); Zechariah Chafee, Jr., *Free Speech in the United States* (1941); and David A. Shannon, *The Socialist Party, A History* (1955).

Several books, none of which is comprehensive, cover the entire period of American demobilization: William E. Leuchtenburg, *The Perils of Prosperity, 1914–1932* (1958); the third volume of Frederick L. Paxson, *The American Democracy and the World War* (1948); Preston W. Slosson, *The Great Crusade and After, 1914–1928* (1930); and James R. Mock and Evangeline Thurber, *Report on Demobilization* (1944). However, the specialized literature on this period is now excellent. David Brody, *Labor in Crisis: The Steel Strike of 1919* (1965), and Philip Taft, *The A.F. of L. in the Time of Gompers* (1957), recount labor's strivings, hopes, and failures. John Hope Franklin. *From Slavery to Freedom: A History of American Negroes* (1967). and Elliot M. Rudwick, *Race Riot at East St. Louis* (1964), detail the travail of American Negroes during this troubled time. For the Red Scare, see Stanley Coben, *A. Mitchell Palmer: Politician* (1963) and his "A Study in Nativism: The American Red Scare of 1919–20," *Political Science Quarterly*, LXXIX (March, 1964), 52–75; Chafee, already cited; Robert K. Murray, *Red Scare: A Study in National Hysteria, 1919–1920* (1955); and William Preston, Jr., *Aliens and Dissenters: Federal Suppression of Radicals, 1903–1933* (1963). For other aspects of unrest, turmoil, and evidences of activities by the "forces of movement," see Robert L. Morlan, *Political Prairie Fire: The Nonpartisan League, 1915–1922* (1955); Theodore Saloutos and John D. Hicks, *Agricultural Discontent in the Middle West, 1900–1939* (1951); Clarke A. Chambers, *Seedtime of Reform, American Social Service and Social Action, 1918–1933* (1963); Aaron I. Abell, *American Catholicism and Social Action* (1960); and Robert M. Miller, *American Protestantism and Social Issues, 1919–1939* (1958).

The literature on the Paris Peace Conference is enormous, and we have space to mention only a few of the works that emphasize the Wilsonian and American contributions. No one should overlook Arno J. Mayer, *Politics and Diplomacy of Peacemaking* (1967), a pioneering work that includes elaborate discussions of the domestic developments that to some degree determined the policies adopted by the peacemakers. Ray Stannard Baker, *Woodrow Wilson and World Settlement* (3 vols., 1922), and Paul Birdsall, *Versailles Twenty Years After* (1941), remain the best long and short works focusing on the deliberations at Paris. But see also Thomas A. Bailey, *Woodrow Wilson and the Lost Peace* (1944); Herbert Hoover, *The Ordeal of Woodrow Wilson* (1958); John M. Thompson, *Russia, Bolshevism, and the Versailles Peace* (1966); and Seth P. Tillman, *Anglo-American Relations at the Paris Peace Conference of 1919* (1961).

For the treaty fight in the United States, see Denna F. Fleming, *The United States and the League of Nations, 1918–1920* (1932); Thomas A. Bailey, *Woodrow Wilson and the Great Betrayal* (1945); James L. Lancaster, "The Protestant Churches and the Fight for Ratification of the Versailles Treaty," *Public Opinion Quarterly*, XXXI (Winter, 1967–1968), 568–596; Wolfgang J. Helbich, "American Liberals in the League of Nations Controversy," *ibid.*, 568–596; Joseph P. O'Grady (ed.), *The Immigrants' Influence on Wilson's Peace Policies* (1967); and the final chapter in Link's *Wilson the Diplomatist*, already cited.

69 70 71   7 6 5 4 3 2 1